Virtue's Alphabet:

From

Amiability to Zeal

By Dr. Donald DeMarco

ISBN 1-887567-20-8

Published by
Central Bureau, Central Verein of America

Printed by
St. Martin de Porres Press
New Hope, KY 40052

Dedication

This book is respectfully dedicated to
Rev. Douglas L. Mosey, CSB
—President-Rector of
Holy Apostles College and Seminary—
whose life and leadership are
lucid examples of
amiability and zeal.

Some of the following chapters have appeared in different versions in the following publications: *Social Justice Review*, *Lay Witness*, *Homiletic & Pastoral Review*, *Celebrate Life*, *Catholic Insight*, *Interim*, *The Catholic Register* (Toronto), *The National Catholic Register*, *Canticle*, and *Gilbert*. The author wishes to thank the editors of these publications for graciously permitting him to reproduce them.

Table of Contents

Preface

Most of us are familiar with the four Cardinal Virtues—Prudence, Justice, Temperance, and Fortitude—and the three Theological Virtues of Faith, Hope, and Love. Yet, for many, the catalogue of virtues ends right there. The fact that there are many more virtues should be welcomed as extremely good news, for the more virtues we develop, the more effective we become as loving persons. It would be comparable to a pianist adding important works to his repertoire, or a pitcher learning to master new pitches.

As an indication of the extensive variety of rich and engaging virtues that exist, I have linked a distinct virtue to each letter of the alphabet, from "amiability" to "zeal". In order to bring these virtues to life, I have presented stories, mostly true-to-life, in which a wide variety of personalities demonstrate how living by virtue is infinitely more attractive and commendable than operating by vice.

The twenty-six virtues that correspond with the letters of the alphabet have an appeal of their own, even apart from up-lifting stories. "Amiability," "Bravery," "Civility," and so on, resonate with a natural glow. They are like so many gems in a jewelry case. On the other hand, the opposite qualities, what are properly called vices, seem ominous. If virtues are attractive, vices are sinister. Consider the catalogue of vices that are the contrasting opposites of our alphabetically ordered virtues: *Aloofness, Timidity, Boorishness, Indecisiveness, Cold-heartedness, Cowardice, Superciliousness, Humorlessness, Cynicism, Injustice, Opportunism, Apathy, Self-centeredness, Covetousness, Willfulness, Trendiness, Heartlessness, Sloth, Duplicity, Intemperance, Ostentation, Mendacity, Foolishness, Dispiritedness, Jadedness,* and *Indifference.*

It is my sincerest hope that this modest work will encourage the reader to pursue virtue more vigorously and shun vice more resolutely. The Media is masterful in making vice seem more attractive than virtue. This is, we might say, its "Cardinal Sin." In reality, however, we yearn to meet people who are models of virtue and fear that we might encounter those who are embodiments of vice. The true value of a book lies in helping us, in some way, to live life well, rather than in offering us an illusory escape from its demands and responsibilities. Inevitably, we must come to terms with life, and the only authentic way to do this is through virtue. And virtue is the lifeblood that allows our love to flow effectively into the lives of others.

Dr. Donald DeMarco
Adjunct Professor
Holy Apostles College
Cromwell, CT
Aug. 15, 2002

Foreword

Angels come and console the martyrs in their prisons and even heal their wounds, like so many good Samaritans; angels are seen taking care of the bodies of Christian athletes, which the persecutor had thrown out to ignominious neglect; angels feed the hermits, and manifest to the early monastic lawgivers what is wise and what is excessive in Christian asceticism; they help the solitary to overcome his terrors at the sight of solitudes filled with evil presences; they give warnings of the approaching death of some lonely servant of God, and they are seen carrying to heaven the soul of many a saint.

Dom Anscar Vonier, in his 1928 book *The Angels*

Contemporary Western civilization is in an age of paganism and intellectual poverty. Angels and virtues are more and more seen as simplicities unworthy of debate and consideration. However, increasingly evident is that with the loss of Western civilizing concepts (such as angels and virtues), individuals become less free, less obligated to their communities and each other, and more enslaved to a Godless destitution with more life not worthy of bragging about much less living. *Virtue's Alphabet: From Amiability to Zeal* reacquaints all with virtues, thereby helping humanity be in the image of God, rather than a brainless, robotile imitation of the latest sensational suggestions from the fraud press and the megamedia. This book is not just a list of simpleminded virtues, but it teaches how to be a genuine human being with or without overt Christianity.

Donald DeMarco, being smarter than most of us, has figured out how to provide a real "How to do it" book! All the other secular "How to do it" books can be put back on the shelves. The author provides the angelic and virtuous foundation for a reclaiming of nature and a conveying of the meaning of civility and decency. This collection of alphabetized virtues is to gain an awareness of genuine "manhood" (virtue) whether male or female. The book fills a void in that it appears that most teachers and parents have abandoned the virtue concept. While William J. Bennett's *The Book of Virtues* and Donald DeMarco's earlier book, *The Heart of Virtue*, helped somewhat, this new work of Dr. DeMarco comes with a friendliness and uplifting dimension on every page. These alphabetized virtues are presented in an instructive way which makes you feel good. Indeed, the entire book is a "feel good!" These deeply moving stories illuminate what real life is all about. This book is a "WOW!"

It has been a long time since I have been instructed so palatably and pleasantly in such a brief period. In fact, the last time I heard anyone formally talk about virtue was a middle-aged priest about 15 years ago at Mass. In his homily, the priest actually talked about "virtue." It sounded foreign because we hear so little of virtue. I have always made it a point, when not totally impossible, to go to the celebrating priest after Mass and say, "Thank you for Mass, Father," and then disappear. This time I gave my "thank you," but also commented that it was refreshing to hear about "virtue" for a change. The priest was genuinely surprised, responding with a broad smile and positive nodding of the head instead of his usual bland "You're welcome."

Today the world has forgotten about virtue when these words are irreplaceable in terms of the creation of a civilized functional human being. Intellectual distortions today result in a massive verbicide of many words, and most young people do not know what these words mean. But not only does this book convey the intellectual meaning but paradigms of action are provided giving life to the word. *Virtue's Alphabet* reinstills an awareness that our purpose in life on one level is "to know, love and serve God in this world so we can be with Him in the next," and at the other level, "to be decent and transcendental whenever possible."

The one chapter on "Empathy" affected me more than the others. This was only because, many years ago, in the early 1960's, I was writing many letters to the United Nations trying to get them to start a special organization for empathy — UNOE

— the United Nations Organization for Empathy. In spite of all my letters, no one ever wrote back. With Don DeMarco's book, I chuckle that it may actually have been a good idea. *Virtue's Alphabet* confirms my theory that "words are angels." St. Thomas Aquinas' second hierarchy in description of angels described the Virtues as those angels involved in the operational effectuation of universal ordering. Whatever angelic Virtues have to do with humans, they involve community aspects and laws. In this regard, Virtues are angels as quanta affirming spacial interactions of genuine Christians. That is, when personal ordered energy is given and taken, Virtues are the angels which especially create prudence in operational dealings. To me, *Virtue's Alphabet* demonstrates that "Virtues as angels" order and structure the identity of genuine humanity leading to Transcendental Love.

The Bible contains many personifications of words. One of my favorites is:

And the Spirit of the Lord shall rest upon Him: The spirit of wisdom and of understanding, the spirit of counsel and of fortitude, the spirit of knowledge and of piety, and he shall be filled with the spirit of the fear of the Lord.

St. Bernard's translation of Isaiah 11:2-3 makes the Gifts of the Holy Spirit to be *spirits* themselves. Words as angels and virtues as Virtues, are spiritual personifications transcendentally communicating spiritual energy as messengers to and from God. Virtues (angels of the Virtue order) enable the operation of transcendentals for all created being in the giving and taking of ordered energy.

Few books are as filled with angelic substance as *Virtue's Alphabet: From Amiability to Zeal*. As I say to all my young patients, "Words are angels, don't you know? Use your words to be a peacemaker instead of a troublemaker." This book reflects the traditional angelic dynamism so needed today. I will read this one to my grandchildren every chance I get. At Christmas, copies will be given to all my children, even though adults. This book will give all an angelic boost.

Samuel A. Nigro, M.D.

Amiability

When *Time* magazine named Pope John Paul II "Man of the Year," in 1994, a small group of its editors and correspondents flew to Rome in order to meet and honor him. After a private audience, Thomas Sancton, chief of correspondents, made the following comment: "I felt something very special in his presence. One does sense that this is no ordinary mortal. There is something about him that surpasses charisma and personality. You don't have to be a Roman Catholic, or even a believer in God, to feel something almost mystical in his presence."

"Charisma" is the Media's favorite word to describe the Pope's magnetic personality. It is a word that has a beautiful genealogy. Derived from the Greek word for grace, *charis*, its original meaning refers to a "release of loveliness." Another word that the Media is fond of employing in describing John Paul II that retains both the root and the rhetoric of the word "charisma," is *amiability*.

Strictly speaking, "charisma" is a gift, whereas "amiability" is a virtue. The latter's etymology goes back to the Latin word for "love" (*amor* – love; *amicitia* – friendship), and its common usage includes a myriad of agreeable qualities, referring to a person who is friendly, good-natured, pleasant, easy to get along with, and warmhearted. Amiability is a resplendent virtue. And one who possesses it is considered gracious, likeable, infectious, uplifting, and impossible to overlook. It has the additional charm of bringing the best out of people, a quality that the American novelist William Makepeace Thackery associated with amiability's charismatic power: "Under the magnetism of friendship the modest man becomes bold; the shy, confident; the lazy, active; or the impetuous, prudent and peaceful."

Pope John Paul II's amiability, indeed, has the salutary

power of bringing the best out of people. This is a most fitting virtue for a Supreme Pontiff to have. It is exactly what is needed to distract people for a moment from his pre-eminent status so that they can feel the warmth of his humanity. When the *Time* magazine delegation was trying to praise the Holy Father as its "Man of the Year" for 1994, the Holy Father, somewhat mischievously, deflected attention from the lofty encomium: "I see that in the past, you have given this honor to Lech Walesa and to Pope John XXIII — but also to Stalin and Hitler." Upon being assured that he was on *Time's* "good list," not its bad one, he replied, gratified, but still in an amiable and playful mood, "I hope I always remain on the good list."

Tad Szulc, in his biography of the Pope, says of his subject that "In public, he likes to joke, often in a slightly self-deprecatory fashion, in whatever language he happens to be using at the time, and enjoys the crowd's laughing, applauding responses. It may be the actor in him." On November 11, 1993, after addressing a group of workers in Rome, he slipped on a newly installed piece of carpeting in St. Peter's Basilica and fell several steps. Though in pain, he said to the crowd on his way out of the hall: "*Sono caduto ma non sono scaduto*" (I have fallen, but I have not been demoted.). The Pope's artificial hip joint that was surgically implanted to compensate for his damaged femur, was giving him some problems. At a synod in October 1994, he looked at the assembled bishops and said, citing the comment Galileo allegedly muttered, "*Eppur' si muove*" (And yet it moves.). Sometimes, when asked how he feels, he would reply, "Neck down, not so good."

In October of 1995, the Pope spoke to a gathering in New York's Central Park about one of his favorite Polish Christmas carols, which he began spontaneously to sing. The large audience roared its approval. John Paul, cocking his head to one side and assuming an expression of surprise, remarked, "And to think — you don't even know Polish." One observer commented that the Pope's gesture was a perfect imitation of Jack Benny.

During a flight from Brussels to Rome (May 21, 1983), a journalist asked His Holiness about the risk of exposing himself to public criticism and objections, he responded by saying, "Even the Pope can learn something." En route to Alaska, the Pope's plane crossed the International Date Line, thereby gaining a calendar year. With a glint of mischief in his eye, John Paul said to his party, "Now we must decide what to do with the extra day we have been given."

Once (August 16, 1972), as Cardinal Wojtyla, he was climbing a mountain when he noticed the darkening skies and heard thunder in the distance. He joked to his guides, "I know three madmen: the first is myself, the second is my secretary, and the third is waiting for us at the summit." A journalist once alerted the Pope of an imminent soccer game to be played between Poland and Italy, and then asked, "which team will you root for?" John Paul responded wisely and humorously: "It would be better for me to keep out of sight."

The late Sir John Gielgud, considered Britain's pre-eminent Hamlet, has remarked that John Paul has a perfect sense of timing. While in Krakow in June of 1979, and being kept up until midnight by an enthusiastic crowd, the Holy Father said to the cheering throng: "You are asking for a word or two, so here they are — Good night." During that same pilgrimage to Poland, a horde of youngsters kept shouting *Sto lat, sto lat* (may you live to a hundred) to the point when John Paul jokingly asked, "How can the Pope live to be a hundred when you shout him down? Will you let me speak?" After order was restored, he simply said, "I love you all."

While in Chicago in October 1979, tens of thousands of Polish-Americans continually serenaded him with *Sto lat*. Finally, John Paul said to them, playfully, "If we keep this up, they're going to think it's the Polish national anthem." To a gathering at Castel Gondolfo (April 17, 1995), John Paul answered repeated shouts of "Long live the Pope," by saying, "Long live everyone."

Someone once remarked, by way of voicing disapproval of Wojtyla's affection for skiing, that no Italian cardinals were skiers. "That's strange, Cardinal Wojtyla said innocently, "in Poland, forty percent of our Cardinals are skiers." His detractor pointedly commented that there were only two Polish Cardinals. "Oh yes," replied Wojtyla, "but in Poland, Cardinal Wyszynski counts for sixty percent." The Holy Father was telling a Polish joke on himself. One of John Paul's biographers, and a close personal friend, John Szostak, has pointed out that John Paul has no objection to Polish jokes as long as they were not cruel. Szostak compiled a list of new Polish jokes for John Paul that was being circulated on the occasion of his elevation to the papacy. One was about the first thing a new Polish Pope would do upon moving in to the Vatican — order wallpaper for the Sistine Chapel.

Szostek treasures a letter that Karol Cardinal Wojtyla sent him two years before they first met, and two years before Wojtyla became Pope John Paul II. It contained a bit of personal advice that Wojtyla always seemed to personify with natural ease: "Always remember, being a person with a good heart and character are the most important virtues in an individual. These qualities will open doors for you and *make life less complicated*." The advice was both practical and memorable, qualities that are intrinsic to amiability.

The day after the Pope gave his Christmas message in 1979, hundreds of Romans returned to St. Peter's square. They began to clap and call for their Pope. John Paul responded by praying the Angelus with them. Then, in a playful mood, said to the throng: "I rejoice with you and I wonder why you have come. Perhaps you came to see if the Pope is at home on the second day of Christmas. And then I think you have come because today is a really beautiful day and attracts one outside. But the Pope has to stay at home because he never knows when people are coming to recite the Angelus. . . . Thank you all and a Merry Christmas to all . . . Blessed be the name of the Lord."

Amiability is a loving heart that expresses itself in a warm smile, a firm handshake, a playful quip, and a charismatic presence. John Paul II is the embodiment of amiability.

Bravery

"Virtue," said Lady Marguerite Blessington, "like a dowerless beauty, has more admirers than followers." The nineteenth century English author, who has a penchant for stating paradoxes, is not being cynical. She is merely observing a fact, one that raises the embarrassing question, "Why is it that we human beings do not imitate what we admire, if not most of the time, at least more often than we do?"

We praise virtue because of its excellence. But we also praise it for its difficulty. Saintliness, the fullness of virtue, is as rare as it is beautiful.

The scene is a park in Calgary, Alberta, on a cold November day. An automobile has broken through a fence, moved over an embankment and plunged into the frigid waters of the Bow River. The driver, a twenty-two-year-old woman by the name of Shannon Roberts, lost control of her vehicle due to a diabetic shock.

Startled onlookers yell to the woman, imploring her to get out of her car. Recognizing that their advice is not being heeded, and sizing up the gravity of the situation, Jeff Liberty goes into action. He strips down to his boxers and dives into the chilling water. Very quickly, he comes in contact with the sinking car. He tries to open the door, but his efforts are in vain. He bangs on the car window and motions the woman to roll it down. She manages to get the window sufficiently lowered so that Jeff can open it the rest of the way. He then proceeds to unfasten her safety belt and eases her through the open window and out to safety.

The ordeal lasted approximately five minutes. The water was deep enough that Jeff never touched bottom. During his life-saving rescue, he recognized that the woman had gone into a deeper state of shock as the water began flooding into the car. He realized that he would have to shoulder the burden of the rescue. When he surfaced and carried the woman to shore, the onlookers along the bank of the river applauded Jeff, as did Canadians across the country, once they read about his daring exploits in the press.

His act, visibly and unmistakably, had all the qualities of bravery. Despite the dangers he faced, he remained attentive and in control. It was a case of "grace under pressure," as Ernest Hemingway once defined this most admirable virtue. There was the element of selflessness, as he focused on the needs of the endangered woman. And there was decisiveness. He knew what needed to be done and he did it – freely, quickly, and effectively.

Jeff Liberty, almost instantly, became a national hero. "What was it like diving into the frigid Bow River, and how could you function so well under such adverse conditions?" This is the question he was obliged to answer again and again. "I guess my adrenaline kind of set in and I didn't really notice the cold anymore," was his modest response.

God equips us with remarkable capacities for doing extraordinary things under difficult circumstances. Our stress response in a time of crisis is far greater than we realize. Bravery in practice releases abilities within ourselves that lie dormant deep within us. Bravery mobilizes them and we surprise ourselves, even "out-do" ourselves, so to speak. Like other virtues, bravery transforms us into a better, larger, more capable human being. Unbidden by bravery, extraordinary human powers remain latent, unexercised, unknown.

Jeff Liberty's story has two further pieces of information that add immeasurably to its charm. He is an Olympic swimmer who represented Canada at the Olympic Games in Sydney, Australia, in the year 2000. The woman was in the first trimester of her pregnancy (the incident has not appeared to harm either her or her unborn child). Canadian readers have feasted on the story. It will be a while before the child, now sleeping quietly in its mother's womb, will be able to appreciate it himself.

But what a story mom has stored in her heart to tell her child one day! Better than any fairy tale – how bravery and a stranger with the improbable name of Liberty, on the day after Remembrance Day, saved both their lives and provided them with the conviction that virtue should be *imitated* in addition to being admired.

Civility

Much has been written and discussed in recent months about the "coarsening of America." The *Jerry Springer Show*, *Temptation Island*, rap lyrics, "raunch radio," X-rated videos, the NBA, XFL, and MTV exemplify how the rude, the crude, and the lewd have become bankable ingredients in the formula for producing good ratings. "Civility," the counteracting virtue to coarseness, seems, by comparison, tame and tepid to many people. Yet civility is the mark of the civilized person. It represents politics at its very best. The coarse and the crude are not exciting as much as they are unpolished and unrefined. They are what we would not do if we only knew better.

In his inaugural address, President Bush made an eloquent and valiant appeal to his fellow citizens to personify civility. With his alliterative promise to lead his country with "civility, courage, compassion, and character," he called attention to civility's primacy. "Sometimes our differences run so deep," the President reminded us, and continuing his alliterative prose, that "it seems we share a continent but not a country." For the philosophically perceptive, the difference between an inhabitant of a continent and a citizen of a country is only too real. It is akin to the difference between *existing* and *flourishing*. But it is a reality that is known only through a spiritual sensibility. Civility, of course, is not a material, economic, or political concept. It is one that is spiritual in its very essence.

Civility is the comportment that distinguishes civilization from barbarism. The barbarian takes what he sees. The citizen works to fulfill a vision. G. K. Chesterton once stated that "Civilization in the best sense merely means the full authority of the human spirit over all externals. Barbarism means the worship of those externals in their crude and unconquered state.

Barbarism is the worship of nature." President Bush is telling us that "A civil society demands from each of us good will and respect, fair dealing and forgiveness." Civility is a virtue that is both broad and deep. It carries within itself the embrace of citizenship and the promise of democracy. The President is appealing to our better angels. He is enjoining us to be "civil," to rise above the prevailing tide of boorishness. He is asking us to be neighborly and just to each other. He is also asking us, when we do meet with abuse and injustice, to be forgiving. He is not naïve about human nature. He knows that barbarity lurks beneath the veneer of civilization and can erupt with shattering force whenever the moral authority of a civilization loses its control.

A much earlier political figure, William Penn, the founder of Pennsylvania, also spoke eloquently about the importance of civility. He understood how a "civil word" can do so much to bring peace and good cheer to citizens. He viewed civility in terms of "lighting another man's candle by one's own, which loses none of its brilliance by what the other gains." Civility does not cost us anything, either in its cultivation or in its expression or in its dispensation. What would cost us dearly would be its omission.

Bush's inaugural address is a virtual treatise on the virtue of civility. "Civility is not a tactic or a sentiment," he warns us. "The insolent civility of a proud man," as the Earl of Chesterfield once remarked, "is, if possible, more shocking than his rudeness could be." True civility is neither presumptuous nor condescending. It is both heartfelt and genuine. It is based on the simple recognition that we are all citizens trying to work together for a common good. Therefore, civility is both realistic and progressive. As the President goes on to explain, "It is the determined choice of trust over cynicism, commitment over chaos."

Cardinal Newman spoke of civilization as "the development of art out of nature, and of self-government out of passion, and of certainty out of opinion, and of faith out of reason." No effort is required to remain cynical, untrusting, and unhopeful. At the same time, no accomplishments can rise from these impoverished attitudes. They are as useless as they are uninspired.

Understanding his role as a moral leader, President Bush culminated his discourse on civility by his personal pledge "to advance my convictions with civility." He will meet with resistance, to be sure, but he promises to respond to them with character and not complaint.

We need *solidarity*, especially when we are opposed by a powerful adversary. We need to express *courtesy* because we all possess a dignity that is a reflection of our Maker. We are commanded to be *neighborly* because we owe each other love. The virtue of *civility*, the least demanding of this quartet of virtues, is based on our shared status as fellow citizens. It asks little, though it promises much. Civility invites communication, enkindles cooperation, releases creativity, and fulfills community. It is a virtue whose noble and distant end is already inherent in its modest and accessible beginning.

Dedication

The last thing that interested Monique Dostie was achieving status as a national celebrity. Her chosen profession seemingly guaranteed that such status would not only be unlikely, but impossible. She had hidden herself away in the sleepy town of Lewiston, Maine, where she operated a small group home for developmentally disabled adults. She lived in the Jaricot Foster Home, as it was called, and offered full-time care for its four residents.

The Home offered quality care to its residents. But also provided a good moral atmosphere. It was precisely the moral values the home honored that led guardians of the residents to place them at the Jaricot Foster Home. There were "rules," to be sure, including the prohibition of sexual activities and the use of pornographic magazines and videos.

Everything was relatively peaceful at this small home. None of the residents—whose level of maturity is comparable to that of 3- to 5-year-olds—ever complained about the rules. But bureaucrats representing the Department of Human Services in the State of Maine were not happy with Ms. Dostie's "rules."

According to DHS rules, mentally retarded and autistic adults who live in a group home have the right to participate in sexual activities of their choice, including viewing pornographic magazines and tapes, and engaging in sexual relations with selected partners. And if the residents want to participate in group sex, the home is obliged to set aside a room specifically for that purpose.

In May of 1998, a war of "rules" began between the Jaricot Foster Home and the Maine Department of Human Services. The state agency urged Monique Dostie to reclassify her "rules" as "guidelines." As a consequence of Dostie's refusal to comply, the state held a hearing at which it ruled that she must comply or face the revocation of her license. Nonetheless, Dostie, a devout Catholic, indicated that she could not, in conscience, betray her wards by exposing them to activities that could be emotionally ruinous to them. According to Ms. Dostie, her developmentally disabled wards cannot handle decisions of daily living, let alone the complex atmosphere that promiscuous sexual relationships would create. Moreover, as Dostie went on to explain, it is not the residents that are requesting sex and pornography, "it's the state that's mandating it." Robert Steinberg, assistant director of licensing and certification with the DHS, stated that residents of group homes may not exercise their sexual rights, but are entitled to them, nonetheless.

With help from a Catholic group, she appealed the decision. In the meantime, the feud between Dostie and DHS began to attract national attention. The June 2, 1999, edition of *The Washington Post*, for example, informed its readers that the Department of Human Services is threatening to cancel the license of this home for mentally retarded adults in Maine unless Monique Dostie agrees to allow sexual activities among her wards.

Joni Fritz, who is the executive director of the American Network of Community Options and Resources representing group homes, has accused Dostie of "denying human sexuality." Curt Decker, executive director of the National Association of Protection and Advocacy Systems for people with disabilities in Washington, has stated that the *biases* of Ms. Dostie should not overtake the *choices* of individuals. Presumably, the Catholic position Dostie holds, no matter how well thought out, is a *bias*, whereas the choices of developmentally disabled individuals, no matter how impetuous, are *self-justifying*.

Dostie, however, remained firm. "I teach that it's wrong [indiscriminate sex], that they don't need that to survive. I teach them their faith and bring God into their lives."

There was considerable public opinion that supported Dostie. Some complained that certain people were denied a license to have a boarding home because they would not permit promiscuous sexual activities. Others complained that they could not find a "sex-free" home where they could lodge their own developmentally disabled children. Some raised the issue of pedophilia, since many adults who are mentally retarded have the emotional maturity of a child.

The appeal, however, did not take place. Thanks to the national attention the dispute had received, agents for a home for the developmentally disabled in Purgitsville, West Virginia, saw in Monique Dostie the kind of person they were looking for. They offered her a position working at their 212-acre mountaintop farm where she would live and work with six mentally retarded adults. Dostie was elated: "Everything we wanted to accomplish was living and well in West Virginia, and looking for help." It all came about "strictly by the providence of God." Dostie will merge the Jaricot Foster Home with the mountaintop operation.

Dedication is an admirable virtue, especially when it is directed to the needs of other people. But its effectiveness cannot be sustained without integrity. When we compromise our dedication—for political, practical, or personal reasons—we compromise the quality of service we provide those to whom we are dedicated.

The members of Maine's Department of Human Services did not object to Ms. Dostie's dedication. It was her integrity that caused them consternation. But Dostie abided accusations of being "unbending," "unrepentant," and "violating the rights of others". And now, thanks to her integrity, she is in a position to dedicate herself to helping more people, and without interference from the State of West Virginia.

Those who are in her care will not think of her as a heroine. They will no doubt think of this 31-year-old woman as did those at her former home, as "Mom". But to outsiders, particularly to Catholics, she is a heroine since she fought an eighteen-month war against powerful bureaucrats and did not allow them to compromise either her dedication or her integrity. She is a heroine because she made sure that virtue triumphed over temptation.

Empathy

Experience may be the sharpest teacher. "One thorn of experience," the poet James Russell Lowell tells us, "is worth a whole wilderness of warning." But only the most insulated individual can learn no other way. More often than not, unfortunately, learning through experience is learning the hard way, getting the test first and the lesson afterward. This explains our penchant for equating "experience" with our mistakes.

Empathy is the intellectual, emotional, and imaginative apprehension of another person's situation that takes place without experiencing it. It is learning through identification, through entering that special matrix where one encounters the unifying "co-humanity" of self and neighbor.

Moments of empathy often arrive unexpectedly and under most unlikely circumstances. I had finished a talk on abortion, some years ago, and was hurrying to get back to my car. It was a cold and rainy October evening. I was tired and anxious to get home. Someone was running after me, calling out my name. He had a story to tell me and neither the time nor the weather nor the setting were going to deter him from his mission. I stopped and listened to him as he unraveled his tale, first with polite indulgence, then with rapt interest.

He had been in Uganda doing peace work as an emissary of the Canadian government. The political situation under Idi Amin had reached a crisis point. My engaging confidante was advised to return to Canada at once.

He boarded a train that would take him out of the country and to freedom. It was his only route out of the jungle. As he soon discovered, he was the only white passenger. A soldier came over to him, pointed a machine gun at his face and contemptuously declared that he could blow him away and not a soul on the train would be at all concerned. For a half-hour, the soldier taunted him, reiterating that any second he might squeeze the trigger and then throw the dead body into the jungle where no one would ever find it.

While the cat and mouse game continued, the other passengers seemed utterly indifferent to my friend's predicament. No one interceded in his behalf. He was an alien in an alien world. His misfortune, which he had no opportunity to avoid, was being in the wrong place at the wrong time and with the wrong people.

In his state of terror, my eager storyteller began to concentrate, with excruciating clarity, on the fragility of his life and on his state of utter helplessness. He waited, without appeal, for the unpredictable judgment of a stranger who wielded an instrument of death. The thirty-minute ordeal, during which time seemed to stand still, finally ended. The soldier withdrew. For whatever reason, unlike Meursault in Camus' *The Stranger*, he chose not to pull the trigger. My friend was reborn. But in that torturous process of rebirth, something extraordinary happened. For a half-hour, he had been completely at the mercy of another person's will. Whether he lived or died hinged solely on someone else's arbitrary choice. And he had survived his appalling ordeal in the damp, womb-like environment of a moving train. All the elements of his experience assisted him in establishing a deep and, what would prove to be, enduring identification with the plight of the unborn. This is why he had to become a lifelong member of the pro-life movement, why he could never be "pro-choice," and why he had to tell me his story.

A sadistic Ugandan soldier had led my friend into the pro-life movement by pointing a machine gun at his head. He had achieved something that countless pro-lifers have failed to achieve through more genteel and civilized attempts at persuasion. Sometimes it is a force other than conventional reason that brings people to see what is at stake in the abortion issue. It may well be that at the heart of the movement is a profound empathic identification with all human beings — those who wait in hope of being rescued, as well as those who wait in silence to be born.

In her autobiography, *It Is I Who Have Chosen You*, Judie Brown recounts her own story about what can be accomplished through empathy. At a time when she was but a neophyte to the art of debating, Mrs. Brown sent a highly distinguished obstetrician/gynecologist scurrying out of the room simply by describing what happens to the unborn during an abortion. The truth that sets us free may first send us running for the exit. As fate (or Providence) would later decree, Judie and her debating opponent were brought together again, though under a much more dramatic set of circumstances. That same pro-abortion doctor was summoned to use his skills in assisting in the difficult and life-threatening birth of Mrs. Brown's third child.

Judie later discovered that the same man she both opposed on the debate floor and welcomed in the delivery room no longer performed abortions. She likes to think that his acquired empathy for the unborn in general and little Christina Brown in particular were instrumental in his change of heart. Empathy has a way of transmitting itself from one person to another in a potentially unending fashion. Empathy is truly an "unending story."

There are two forms of intelligence. One is of the mind, the other of the heart. In the moral sphere there can be no doubt that the empathy of the heart is incomparably more important than the photography of the mind. Through the mind we can know and understand, but through the heart we can love, serve, and change the world.

Fortitude

Any writer or film director, these days, living in complete comfort and security, who produces a *risqué* work that causes a flutter of excitement among art critics is applauded for his "courage." It is never clear, however, what great good he is defending or what grave evil he is facing. This popular demotion of courage to mere sensationalism (or fortitude to fashion) illustrates our contemporary vulgarization of virtue. "Courage" is sometimes nothing more than irreverence, while sentimentality often passes for "compassion" and mere stubbornness masquerades as "integrity."

Fortitude is a virtue of heroic and even supernatural dimensions. It is the fourth of the gifts of the Holy Spirit and corresponds to the Fourth Beatitude, "Blessed Are They That Hunger And Thirst After Justice." Fortitude deals with lofty goods and formidable dangers.

St. Thomas Aquinas refers to fortitude as "a certain firmness of mind" which "is required both in doing good and in enduring evil, especially with regard to goods or evils that are difficult" (*Summa Theol.* II-II, Q 139, a.1). He goes on to say that "man's mind is moved by the Holy Ghost in order that he may attain the end of each work begun, and avoid whatever perils may threaten." Fortitude is courage that transcends itself through supernatural assistance.

Baroness Catherine de Hueck Doherty, foundress of Madonna House in Combermere, Ontario, and life-long friend of the poor and the marginalized, is a lady of true fortitude.

Many years ago, the Jesuits of Fordham University in the Bronx, New York, tried assiduously to convince her that they could not accept black students. Over a three- decade period, the persistent Baroness had presented the university with highly qualified and capable black candidates. Though these candidates had high school averages over 90%, were good athletes, and were certified by their parish priests as being daily communicants, Fordham routinely and resolutely refused to admit them.

Despite their long-standing disagreement, the Jesuits once invited her to lecture at their school. Faculty and students filled the hall. She walked onto the stage and spoke these words: I came to talk to you, not to lecture. In 10 minutes, therefore, I am stepping off this platform. Ten minutes is no lecture, as far as I am concerned. The situation here is very tragic. You have a chapel in this building, and there is a crucifix in the chapel. This same cross shines all over New York. However, the words of the person who died on that cross are ignored in these holy precincts.

She then named one of the young men she had presented to the university. "According to your teachers," she continued, the administration has turned thumbs down on his admittance here. They have told me that you do not want undergraduate Negroes. That's why I am getting off this platform right now."

Fortitude is an engaging virtue. And when it shines from a stage, and comes directly from the heart, unrehearsed, it can prove overpowering. "No, don't go," the audience chanted. "Talk to us! Talk to us!" The Baroness talked, and in her own humble estimation, delivered what she thought was the best lecture on interracial justice she ever gave. Once she finished her impromptu remarks, someone rose and challenged the school to change its admission policy. Unanimous cries of "Yes! Yes!" filled the room. "Thank you," said the Baroness de Hueck. "I am sure God is here tonight."

She had embarrassed and disturbed her Jesuit hosts. She was a force, in their opinion, that needed to be quelled. Some time later, Fordham's president and about 20 of his priestly colleagues spoke to her behind closed doors. "Baronness," one pleaded with her, "you realize, don't you, that many of our students are from the South. If we accept a Negro there will be a great hullabaloo among the parents and the students." "The time is not yet ripe," commented another priest.

The Baroness was equipped with fortitude, but she also made sure to bring with her a 25-cent Bible marked by ribbons at the appropriate texts. "I have never read anywhere in the Gospel where Christ says to wait 20 years before living the Gospel. The Good News is for now. He died for all men, to make all men his brothers and sisters, children of his Father." "But we will go broke," protested another.

"It's a question of what you're more interested in," the Baroness retorted, "God or mammon. God said you cannot have two masters."

Fortitude can be a lonely virtue. For nearly two hours, the Jesuits badgered her with objections. Truth, justice, love, faith, fortitude, and conscience make a formidable alliance, even though they may take up residence in a solitary heart. *Status quo* is a logjam. Fortitude is a progressive force. Though it may be misread as imprudent, it is in the final analysis, essential for the advance of human civilization.

Graciousness

Human beings are equal in dignity, but unequal in talent, status, and reputation. Because the marks of inequality are more conspicuous than dignity, which is a spiritual quality, they often determine and dominate human relationships. Birds of a feather, or men of the same stripe, tend to congregate exclusively. Some ballplayers who define themselves in terms of their batting average will not dine with colleagues who hit below .300. In some circles it is an unequivocal sign of success that a businessman is not obligated to return his phone calls.

Graciousness is the virtue that counts human dignity to be infinitely more important than the more conspicuous features of talent, status, or reputation. The supreme example of graciousness is Christ who not only answers prayers, but also makes house calls. He shares His Life with us as the center of the Mystical Body. And he invites us to share in that Life, not in virtue of what distinguishes us, but in virtue of what unites us — our common humanity.

Placing the marks of distinction above the dignity of one's humanity, commonplace as it is, can be vain and unattractive. The secular world, having lost sight of human dignity, is sycophantically disposed to laud what elevates the individual. A certain hockey player is ceremoniously called "The Great One" for no other reason than his prolific ability to score points on the ice. A particular boxer proclaims, "I am the Greatest," merely because of his pugilistic prowess in the ring.

A friend of mine, who is a registered nurse in Connecticut, was involved in organizing a pro-life conference. "If we had a big name," she said to her co-workers, "we'll draw more people." And so, with little appreciation for protocol or practicality, she called Cardinal O'Connor's office and invited His

Eminence to be a guest speaker. An office secretary assured her that the invitation would be passed on to New York City's very busy archbishop.

Several days passed. One evening, when my friend was spending a leisurely evening at home, the phone rang. "Hello, is this Mary Smith? This is Cardinal O'Connor." My friend leapt to her feet and her mind sprang to attention. "It really is him," she thought to herself. "Thank you for inviting me to speak at your pro-life conference, but it seems that I have another engagement that day." She could hear the pages of his schedule book fluttering as he turned to the date in question. He seemed apologetic about having to speak at the United Nations that day and therefore would not be able to accept Mary's invitation. "But," he added, "I want you to know that what you are doing is very important and that I will pray for the success of your conference." The conference was a success, though, my friend still can't get over her own *chutzpah*.

The first time I encountered Cardinal O'Connor was in Washington, D.C. at a pro-life conference in 1985. He had just returned from Rome and was holding his newly acquired red hat in his hands. "Put it on," people clamored. His modest retort: "It doesn't fit."

Eight years later, after I spoke at Dunwoodie Seminary in Yonkers, New York, an aide informed me that, "The Cardinal wants to see you." "What would I say to him?" I thought to myself. To establish a common bond at the outset, I mentioned a friend of mine who came all the way from Moose Jaw, Saskatchewan, to New York City hoping to join his newly created order, "Sisters of Life." To my astonishment, the Cardinal remembered her name and even the details of her situation. I was in the presence of graciousness personified.

As Archbishop of New York, Cardinal O'Connor launched several programs for people with AIDS, inaugurated annual celebrations with people with disabilities, promoted workers' causes, and formed three religious orders. He deemed his military pension more than enough to live on and therefore refused any salary or stipends as archbishop. In 1988 he donated all his

Social Security earnings for the rest of his life to a scholarship fund he started for African-American students.

He lived by the simple maxim, as he once told an interviewer that, "the disciple cannot be greater than the master." Christ said to all his future followers: "As the world has hated me, so the world will hate you." "If there is any meaning at all to the fact that a bishop is an apostle of Christ," he explained, "it is in these words."

Surely John O'Connor was a man of title: in addition to "priest," "archbishop," and "cardinal," he earned several academic degrees including a "doctorate" in political science from Georgetown University and, after 27 years as military chaplain, retired as "Navy chief of chaplains" with the rank of "rear admiral."

But he will be remembered most of all for his graciousness. He submerged his titles so that they would never interfere with his common touch. He was a human among humans. None of us should aspire to be anything more than that.

Humor

Barbara Bush, daughter of President George W. Bush, completed her freshman year at Yale in May of 2001. Her great grandfather, Senator Prescott Bush, as well as her presidential grandfather, and her father all earned degrees from that same hallowed institution. Yet, the fact that four generations of the Bush family tree had graced Yale with their presence did nothing to ingratiate the sitting president with many of the school's faculty and graduating students when he was asked to speak during commencement exercises.

Upon receiving an honorary doctorate of laws degree and standing before the graduating class of 2001, on May 21, President Bush was greeted with a raucous fusillade of boos. Hundreds of yellow signs conveyed messages protesting his policies and positions on a number of issues. More than 200 faculty members had signed a petition objecting to his appearance. One of them, Peter Brooks, said that President Bush has been in office too briefly. "He's still a cipher," said Professor Brooks.

Well, not quite net zero. He would be clever enough, at any rate, to dull the sting of all the outrageous epithets which rebellious students were hurling at him with disarming humor. "Grow Trees No Bushes." "Execute Justice Not People." "Oh no Gore's ahead, better call my brother Jeb!" "Protect Reproductive Rights." Some wore mortarboards with models of coal-fired utility plants belching puffs of smoke. They turned their backs to him when he began speaking. All in all, not exactly expressions of kindness or civility. Certainly nothing like the standing ovation the students gave Hillary Rodham Clinton twenty-four hours earlier on Class Day.

The three most contentious issues that mobilized the unhappy Elies were the environment, abortion, and the current

AIDS policy. It was as if the protestors were insisting that nature should remain natural and not serve man, while sex should become unnatural and not serve life.

How does one encounter such a stormy sea of angry protest? With reasoned argumentation, yards of statistics, persuasive rhetoric? President Bush took the wiser route. He chose to disarm his opponents with self-deprecating humor. If he could survive his more pointed self- administered barbs, how could he be harmed by the tamer assaults of his adversaries?

"To the 'C' students," he said with a grin, "I say you, too, can be president of the United States." "I know Yale has a tradition of having no commencement speaker. I also know that you've carved out a single exception . . . Now you have to be a Yale graduate, you have to be a president and you have to have lost the Yale vote to Ralph Nader." He noted that Dick Cheney dropped out of Yale and joked that this explained why he had to settle for being vice-president. His witticisms drew laughter, even from his antagonists.

"My critics don't realize I don't make verbal gaffes," he quipped, referring to an esoteric course in Japanese poetry he took while at Yale, "I'm speaking in the perfect form and rhythms of ancient haiku." He later added, "Everything I know about the spoken word, I learned right here at Yale."

The prodigal son had returned. He had told associates during his presidential campaign that Yale was a fount of intellectual and liberal elitism. In this matter, he was merely speaking the truth. Nonetheless, Yale deconstructionists, themselves, did not want to be either deconstructed or exposed. There are some things that even deconstructionists do not want deconstucted. Yet, the President was neither confrontational nor penitent. He was congratulatory and reached out to those who disagreed with him. He disarmed with his humor and charmed with his humanity. He exploited (if we can use this term in a positive sense) the protestors to his own advantage.

Lighthearted humor in the face of opposition is a virtue of great practical value. It presupposes a host of other virtues: humility, courage, and self-possession. And it anticipates friendship and collegiality. A president need not be solemn to appear presidential. Well-paced humor, especially that which is directed at one's self, indicates an awareness of one's imperfections. At the same time, it indicates a sturdy enough character that does not allow imperfections to be a source of discouragement.

Humor is not only enjoyable; it is infectious. It sets a tone of humility and invites people to relate to each other on a human level, rather than one which is merely political, social, or academic.

President Bush's return to his *alma mater* provoked controversy. But it showed that the nation's new leader could rise above controversy and respond to it with cordiality. A clear victory for the President! And a commencement lesson that his protestors would be wise to absorb.

Innocence

The distinguished Catholic convert, Monsignor Ronald Knox, said of G. K. Chesterton that his good friend possessed two virtues in particular, innocence and humility. There are exceedingly few contemporary writers to whom the same ascription could be honestly applied. This unusual combination of virtues, however, is of inestimable value to the writer, for it allows him to see things as they are rather than how he would prefer them to be. But it is also of great value for the Christian who seeks to accomplish God's will rather than his own.

We usually think of innocence not as a virtue, but as a condition of the very young who are not yet aware of evil in the world. In *Life is Beautiful*, The Best Foreign Film of 1999, a father endears himself to audiences by the loving and imaginative ways in which he protects his son from a premature awareness of the evil of racism.

In one scene, the son notices a sign on a door saying, "No Jews or dogs allowed." The boy asks his father why they are not allowed to go in. The father, understanding that there are some realities that a defenseless child cannot face, makes light of the situation. "Everybody does what he wants to do," he says. "There's a hardware store where they don't allow Spaniards or horses." Somewhat confused, his son says, "But we let everybody into our bookstore." "From now on, we'll have a sign, too," replies THE FATHER. "IS THERE ANYBODY YOU DON'T LIKE?" "SPIDERS," HIS son answers, "what about you?" "I don't like Visigoths," states the father, emphatically and without hesitation. "From now on we'll have a sign that says, "No spiders or Visigoths allowed."

The father cleverly reduces anti-Semitism to an unaccountable eccentricity, thereby protecting his son's innocence. Barring spiders and Visigoths (a branch of Goths that settled in France and Spain in the fifth century) seems, to the child, more playful than prejudicial.

The word innocent literally means, free from harm (*nocere* in Latin refers to harm, as in the medical axiom, *Primum non nocere* — First do no harm. The innocence of the child is freedom from an awareness of evil. It is with this latter sense in mind that Shakespeare asked, "What is a stronger breastplate than a heart untainted?"

The importance of the *virtue* of innocence is implied in Christ's admonition: "I tell you solemnly, unless you change and become little children you will never enter the kingdom of heaven" (Mt 18:03).

The child is free from an awareness of sin. Christ is telling us that we must remain childlike in the sense that we do not adapt to sin. To acquire the virtue of innocence means to remain childlike in adulthood without sacrificing our developed awareness of sin. It is the innocence of Saint Francis of Assisi in his Sermon to the Birds.

Innocent Smith is a creation of Chesterton. But he also embodies the innocence of its author. He represents, according to Msgr. Knox, "the innocence and the fresh eyes of childhood, investing with excitement and color the drab surroundings—or so they have seemed hitherto—of half a dozen unsuccessful and disillusioned people." Innocent Smith is youth-reborn, childlikeness recaptured. He displays the virtue of innocence to a world that has grown dull with sinfulness.

Chesterton would not have possessed the virtue of innocence had he not also possessed the virtue of humility. Innocence protects us from the poison from without; humility protects us from the poison from within. Pride, our most toxic inner poison, causes our vision of ourselves and reality to be blurred, primarily because it leads us to take ourselves too seriously and reality not seriously enough. It is, as Chesterton states rather succinctly, "the falsification of fact by the introduction of self." If a person is truly to learn anything at all, he must first "subtract *himself* from the study of any solid and objective thing."

There are cynics who see nothing of value. There are fanatics who see nothing other than themselves to be of value. Innocence allows us to see value wherever it exists. Humility prevents us from perverting them for our own use. Chesterton said that he was never interested in mirrors. By that, he meant that he was never interested in his own reflection or reflections. His entire attitude was outward. He exulted with the saints in being a child of creation.

Humility gives us a clean window; innocence gives us a clear vision. Together they allow us to see the world that God has put before our senses:

All my mental doors open outwards into a world I have not made. My last door of liberty opens upon a world of sun and solid things, of objective adventures. The post in the garden; the thing I could neither create not expect; strong plain daylight on stiff upstanding wood; it is the Lord's doing and it is marvellous in our eyes (*The Uses of Diversity*).

Innocence and humility are liberating virtues. They are not the virtues of the secular world, but they are virtues of the child of God who is advancing cheerfully toward his heavenly destiny.

Justice

The name Jérôme Lejeune is well known to Canadian pro-lifers. The distinguished geneticist crossed the Atlantic several times to reassure Canadian audiences that science has, indeed, established that life begins at conception when sperm fertilizes egg. His most notable appearance was as an expert witness for the humanity of the unborn during the Joe Borowski "Trial of the Century." There, he testified that "At the moment of fertilization the whole symphony of life is ready to be played out." When the defense counsel asked him whether his Roman Catholicism had influenced his views, he stated that he opposed abortion because he is a geneticist and a scientist.

Life is a Blessing is a memoir and an accolade from the pen of the youngest of his four daughters and five children. There can be no more touching tribute for a father than to be praised by his children, especially by a daughter. "How does one write a book about one's father?" Clara asks in her Preface. "His life is at the same time too near and too far for the solemnity of the usual biography. Too near because affection can scarcely maintain a critical point of view; too far because his story is not ours, even though we are, from a certain moment on, intimately involved in it."

Clara's account of her father's life and dedication to the sick and the handicapped is told from the heart, as it should be, coming from his daughter. But there is a second reason for the appropriateness of the heart. Lejeune, although a scientist of world-class distinction, fully understood the importance of the heart. "Our intelligence is not just an abstract machine," he wrote, "it is also incarnate, and the heart is as important as the faculty of reason, or more precisely, reason is nothing without the heart."

That Lejeune's heart was never dissociated from his scientific intelligence is a *leitmotiv* that characterizes the essence of his life. Lejeune carved his niche in history's pantheon of science when he discovered the genetic cause—trisomy 21—of Downs Syndrome. One day a popular television program in France, "*Un dossier de l'écran* ("On Screen Dossier"), aired a debate on the question of aborting unborn children who had trisomy 21. The debate put terror in the hearts of both Downs Syndrome children as well as their parents. The next day, a ten-year-old boy with trisomy arrived at Lejeune's office for consultation. He was crying inconsolably. As his mother explained, "He watched the debate last night." The child threw his arms around Dr. Lejeune's neck and said to him, "They want to kill us. You've got to defend us. We're just too weak, and we don't know how." "From that day on," Clara reports, "Papa would untiringly come to the defense of the pre-born child."

There is no doubt that Lejeune was a man of compassion. But he was also a man of justice. He understood as a man and as a scientist that it is gravely unjust to kill any member of the human family, born or unborn. Socrates, as Plato records in his dialogue, *Gorgias*, taught that it is better to suffer an injustice than to commit one. When we commit an injustice, we suffer a contamination in our soul. We can endure injustices against us without losing our integrity. But our integrity is sullied the moment we execute our first act of injustice.

Lejeune lived in accordance with this Socratic dictum. To be just, and oppose the injustice of abortion is far greater than to seek social approval while ignoring the just claims of the unborn to live. His abiding sense of justice is evident in a statement he made in *Lancet* in opposing the medical non-treatment of Down's syndrome babies:

Those who delivered humanity from plague and rabies were not those who burned the plague-stricken alive in their houses or suffocated rabid patients between two mattresses. Health by death is a desperate mockery of medicine.

Victory against Down's syndrome – i.e., curing children of the ill-effects of their genetic overdose – may not be too far off, if only the disease is attacked, not the babies.

Lejeune's commitment to the unborn remained passionate and unswerving throughout his life. It often required great courage, however, and exacted many personal sacrifices. On one occasion, during a debate at the *Mutualité*, he was hit in the face with raw calves' liver and tomatoes. Another time, took the podium at the United Nations and decried their professed sympathy for abortion. "Here we see an institute of health that is turning itself into an institute of death." That evening, writing to his wife, he confided, "This afternoon I lost my Nobel Prize." Political correctness, to be sure, held absolutely no attraction for Lejeune. To suffer injustice was always preferable to him than committing it.

But his pro-life commitments created problems for his family members as well. Clara recalls that when she was twelve or thirteen years of age, she and her sister, when riding their bicycles past the walls of the medical school, were horrified to find the following ominous threats painted in black letters: "Tremble, Lejeune! The MLAC [a revolutionary student movement] is watching." "Lejeune is an assassin. Kill Lejeune." "Lejeune and his little monsters must die."

Lejeune never descended to the vulgarity of fighting people. "I am fighting false ideas," he would say. If he was fighting at all, he was fighting *for* people. Yet that was enough to make him the target of angry attackers. He became, as his daughter tells us, "the object of unconscious fury on the part of those who set themselves up as the apostles of tolerance." The litany of persecutions and discriminations her suffered was extensive, and yes, to use that tired word, "incredible."

Clara and her siblings bore the stigma of being the children of Professor Jérôme Lejeune. They learned, rather painfully, that "we have to live with labels that don't define us." It was, as Clara describes it, a new kind of "original sin."

Dr. Lejeune maintained his deep concern for the suffering even when he, himself, was near death and suffering acutely from both the cancer that finally killed him and the massive chemotherapy he was undergoing. As his daughter testifies, he would answer the telephone while exhausted, between bouts of vomiting, in order to discuss a therapeutic hypothesis with a colleague. "His suffering was intolerable at times," writes Clara, "but he was always considerate of others; he put himself in their place." During his last days, when what little strength he had was ebbing from his body, he identified with the motto of the Roman Legionary, "*Et si fellitur de genu pugnat*" (And if he should fall, he fights on his knees). For Lejeune, life, justice, compassion, and service were all inseparably intertwined.

He passed away, in accord with a presentiment he had, on Easter Sunday, April 3, 1994. Pope John Paul II delivered a eulogy the next day in which he referred to "our brother Jérôme," and stated that "If the Father who is in heaven called him from this earth on the very day of Christ's Resurrection, it is difficult not to see in this coincidence a sign."

Lejeune and the Holy Father were close friends. Professor Lejeune and his wife had enjoyed lunch with the Pope on that near fatal day of May 13, 1981 when an assassin's bullet rang out in Vatican Square. That very night, Lejeune experienced stomach pains so severe that he was taken by an ambulance to a hospital. "No one understood what was wrong," writes his daughter, "and he experienced the pain of the Pope's wound." He would have surgery, as did the Holy Father. Their temperature curves were similar, and they left the hospital on the same day. Was it a "coincidence"? Was it a "God-incident"? Or was it the result of a powerful bond between spiritual brothers that passes understanding?

Lejeune could never do enough for his patients. Two images provided him with recurring guidance and inspiration. The first is the final line from Brahms' *Requiem*: "Blessed are those who die in the Lord. For their works follow them." Lejeune's compassionate work continues under the auspices of "La Foundation Jérôme Lejeune" which was established in his name to continue his research into the causes and treatments of mental handicaps. The second is St. Vincent de Paul's reply when the Queen asked him, "What must one do for one's neighbor?" "More!"

Kingliness

Agesilaus II, King of Sparta in the fourth century B. C., compared his kingly role to that of a good father. "The king will best govern his realm who reigneth over his people as a father doth over his children." "Royalty," he added, "consists not in vain pomp, but in great virtues."

This manner of understanding the exercise of kingship in relation to specific virtues was not unusual for the ancients, who regarded the king as the antithesis of the tyrant. Thus we find in the writings of St. Isidore in the seventh century, these words: "Whence there was this proverb among the ancients: You will be king if you do right; but you will not be if you do not. The royal virtues are principally two: justice and piety."

This ancient tradition disposed Christians to accept Christ, "King of the Jews," as their king (Mt 27:11; Mk 15:2; Lk 23:3). Christ perfectly integrates the kingly virtues of leadership and service. As Aquinas writes in *The Governance of Rulers*: "The idea of king implies that he be one man who is chief and that he be a shepherd who seeks the common good of the multitude and not his own advantage."

Properly speaking, only a king can exercise the virtues peculiar to kingship. Christ the King exemplifies the virtues of justice and piety, leadership and service. These are paradoxical pairings since it often happens that a man of justice is severe, and a leader is egoistic.

Throughout history, kings have often failed miserably in living up to the virtues proper to their office. Yet the virtue of kingliness is real, and when personified, becomes exceedingly beautiful. King Boudewijn of Belgium is a case in point.

Boudewijn was born near Brussels in 1930, the elder son of King Leopold III and Queen Astrid. He became king of Belgium in 1951, the day after his father abdicated, and two months before his 21ˢᵗ birthday. A faithful Catholic and noted for his piety (he was a daily communicant), King Boudewijn was appalled when the Belgian Parliament approved a bill, in 1990, widening the availability of abortion. Rather than sign his name to the bill, which was expected of him, he resigned his kingship. He could not, in conscience, ratify a law that consigned any of his subjects to an unjust and unnecessary death. He saw his kingly role as leader and servant extending to everyone in his kingdom, born and unborn.

His abdication made world headlines. But there was an unexpected consequence to his action, no less worthy of publicity, that the Media ignored.

When the distinguished philosopher, Alice von Hildebrand, a native of Belgium, learned of Boudewijn's selfless and courageous act, she dispatched a letter of praise to him, telling him how his noble gesture made her proud to be a Belgian citizen. In due time, Dr. von Hildebrand received a thank you note from the king's secretary. Discussing the matter with co-patriots, she was surprised and pleased to learn that a great number of Belgians throughout the world had similarly praised their king for his selfless defense of innocent human life. And then she learned, as Paul Harvey is wont to say, "the rest of the story."

The king's secretary was a young woman who was scheduled to have an abortion. Each day, prior to her date with the abortionist, she would come in to work, open and read mail that poured in from all over the world paying tribute to her king and the little child that sleeps within its mother's womb. Each letter she read and each thank you note she dispatched was an affirmation of life and a refutation of abortion. They were also affirmations of her noble king whose kingliness had touched her, and in touching her, blessed the life she was carrying. As she sat in her office, day after day, processing mail, she was exquisitely situated between her king and her life within. Only a few inches separated her royal stationary from her unborn child. At last, pro-life Belgians throughout the world finally convinced her that there was no *moral* distance between her king and her child. She was, as it were, carrying her own little king. Her role as corresponding secretary was indeed salutary. She changed her mind and cancelled the abortion. Perhaps without realizing it, she was sending another and more effective kind of letter out to the world, her own special tribute to her king in the most perfect way possible, not merely by praising life, but by giving birth to it.

Love

There is no other word in our language that is more abused, misused, and confused than the word "love." Yet its essential meaning is not difficult to understand. The weight of the entire Christian tradition tells us, quite simply, that love is a tendency toward the real. St. Francis de Sales, in his *Treatise on the Love of God* expresses it more poetically when he states, "Love is the movement, effusion and advancement of the heart toward the good."

Love overcomes separation and intimately unites us with reality. In its interpersonal manifestation, it affirms the reality of the beloved, that is to say, his or her truth, goodness, and desirability. "Love is not blind," G. K. Chesterton remarks in his *Orthodoxy*, "that is the last thing it is. Love is bound; and the more it is bound, the less it is blind." Love is bound to the reality of the beloved, a reality that is fundamentally true, good, and desirable. Love does not build castles in the air. It establishes sturdy foundations.

In this regard, it is an easy matter to recognize love and to distinguish it from its legion of counterfeits. Love passes through three stages. It is *attentive*, *appreciative*, and *affectionate*. By paying attention, we focus on the truth of the other person. We listen with love as we tune in to the truth of the other, the truth that the other is trying to express, however clumsily that expression might be rendered. By showing appreciation, we indicate that we value the other as fundamentally good. Love shows appreciation by affirming the goodness of the other. Affection is love expressing itself by rejoicing in the desirability of the other. Gifts, touches, smiles, sacrifices, and favors, are among the many ways in which love demonstrates its affection and affirms the desirability of the other. It crowns its recognition of the other's truth and goodness.

The opposite of love is not hate, but apathy. No one wants to be ignored, disregarded, or neglected (the polar opposites of receiving attention, appreciation, and affection). People want their truth to be heard, their goodness to be cherished, and their desirability to be felt. They want their reality affirmed, honored, and embraced. They want to be loved. And just as true as it is that all people want to be loved, all people want to express love.

The progression from attention to appreciation to affection is important. Wisdom always places things in the right order. This order represents the proper development of love. We are not showing love if we express affection for someone whose truth and goodness are unknown to us. Love begins with knowledge of the other. *Ubi amor, ibi oculus* (wherever there is love, there is knowledge). This knowledge uncovers the truth and the goodness of the other. Affection without personal knowledge does not serve the other, but is more likely to be an act of impetuosity.

Love, therefore, must be patient as it advances from attention to appreciation to affection. Love takes time. Love at first sight is less likely than like at first look. When we sense that we like another person, we should then be patient and temperate enough to get to know the truth and appreciate the good of that person so that our affection will be founded on something real.

Love does justice to the beloved and does not ascribe to the beloved values that do not exist. Love is not a romantic projection or a tantalizing illusion. It is the affirmation and promotion of the real person who is the recipient and the beneficiary of our love.

Therefore, love embraces a variety of virtues. This includes not only patience, temperance, and justice, but also hope, courage, and fidelity. The more virtues we have, the better prepared we are to love. Love is the form of all virtues, and virtues are the indispensable conduits of love.

The meaning of love is simple enough not to elude us but the simplicity of its meaning does not imply any frequency of its occurrence. We should be artful when it comes to loving, and circumspect when it comes to recognizing that we are loved. We all need to love and to be loved, but we should not want to settle for any of its imposters.

Martyrdom

Martyrdom is the supreme witness given to the truth of faith. It means bearing witness to the faith even unto death. The very etymology of the word (*martyros* in Greek) means *witness*. The martyr accepts this death with courage as a witness to the faith and to the presence of the Kingdom of God.

The well known writer, Norman Cousins, once denounced "any man in the pulpit who by his words and acts encourages his congregation to believe that the main purpose of the church or the synagogue is to provide social respectability for its members." This denunciation resonates well with secular society's general intolerance of preaching the Word of God to promote the image of a "holier-than-thou" social respectability.

The most definitive contradiction of "religion as hypocrisy" is *martyrdom*. The fact of martyrdom is the ultimate and unequivocal witness, not of the world or of the self, but of God. It is the price that must be paid to silence the detractors and make the presence of God known to a world of skeptics.

Franz Jägerstätter is a martyr for our modern world whose witness should be more widely known. Initially, a martyr, such as Jägerstätter, may be a "solitary witness." But there is no limit to the number of people who can be witness to his witness. Jägerstätter's witness might have remained virtually solitary except for the witness of another — Catholic sociologist Gordon Zahn. It was Zahn, a University of Massachusetts professor, who discovered Jägerstätter's inspiring story of courage and unyielding commitment to God, and brought it to light in his book, *In Solitary Witness* (1964). The book has now been translated into several languages, including German, French, Italian, and Greek.

Franz Jägerstätter was born in 1909 in St. Radegund, a

small village in Upper Austria about thirty kilometers from Braunau-am-Inn, the birthplace of Adolph Hitler. In 1936 he married a woman from a nearby village, and the two went to Rome for their honeymoon. A Catholic by birth, Franz experienced a spiritual re-awakening of his faith around the time of his marriage and served his parish church in the capacity of a sexton.

On March 11, 1938, Hitler's forces crossed into Austria and two days later incorporated it into *Grossdeutschland*. In due time, the invaders presented Jägerstätter and all the other ablebodied men of St. Radegund, their orders to swear allegiance to Hitler and serve in the Nazi army. Jägerstätter alone, refused to comply. He was a Catholic, and in conscience could neither honor or serve the evil purposes of an intrinsically immoral political regime. He refused, knowing that his refusal would cost him his life. The drama, in the words of Professor Zahn, was "nothing less than a repetition of an old story, the ever-recurring confrontation between Christ and Caesar."

Jägerstätter was also married and a father to his wife's three little girls. He was also urged by many of his neighbors to be "prudent" and not risk his life by offending the Nazis. But Jägerstätter was resolved. While in prison and awaiting execution, he wrote: "Again and again people stress the obligations of conscience as they concern my wife and children. Yet I cannot believe that, just because one has a wife and children, he is free to offend God by lying (not to mention all the other things he would be called upon to do). Did not Christ Himself say, 'He who loves father, mother, or children more than Me is not deserving of My love'?" Just a few hours before his death, he stated in a letter to his family, "I will surely beg the dear God, if I am permitted to enter heaven soon, that he may also set aside a little place in heaven for all of you."

On August 9, 1943, in a Berlin prison, Franz Jägerstätter, like Saint Thomas More, was beheaded.

The night before the execution, a Fr. Jochmann visited Jägerstätter in his cell. The priest found the prisoner, who had already received the last sacraments earlier that day, completely calm and prepared. The opportunity to avoid death was still available. On the table before him lay a document that Jägerstätter had only to sign in order to have his life spared. When the priest called his attention to it, Jägerstätter provided a simple explanation: "I cannot and may not take an oath in favor of a government that is fighting an unjust war."

Jägerstätter remained calm and composed when he walked to the scaffold. On that very same evening, Fr. Jochmann said, in the company of a group of Austrian nuns: "I can only congratulate you on this countryman of yours who lived as a saint and has now died a hero. I say with certainty that this simple man is the only saint that I have ever met in my lifetime."

Jägerstätter died convinced that his manner of death would pass unnoticed by the world and would completely fade from human memory with the passing of the handful of people who had known him personally. He was a martyr, not a prophet. In December 1984, responding to a nationwide petition, the President of Austria formally issued a special posthumous Award of Honor to Franz Jägerstätter. At the Second Vatican Council, an English Archbishop called upon his fellow bishops "to consider this man [Franz Jägerstätter] and his sacrifice in a spirit of gratitude" and let his example "inspire our deliberations." The document that issued from these deliberations would be eventually known as *The Pastoral Constitution on the Church in the Modern World.*

Neighborliness

Philip Van Doren Stern is hardly a household name. Yet a short story he penned on the back of a Christmas card provided moviemaker Frank Capra with material for a cinematic classic that has won an honored place in the homes and hearts of countless televiewers each year at Christmas time. When Capra first read Stern's "The Greatest Gift: A Christmas Tale," he exclaimed, "That's the story I've been looking for all my life." He produced, from his long sought after story, "It's A Wonderful Life." As a work of art, it has been favorably compared to Charles Dickens' "A Christmas Carol." As a film, it won five Academy Award nominations. As a heartwarming story, it has become widely esteemed as *the* Christmas movie.

The story centers on a good man who, because of financial difficulties, finds himself at the end of his tether. He decides to do away with himself. In Stern's original story, George Pratt, in his moment of desperation, cries: "I'm stuck here in this mudhole for life — a small-town bank clerk. I never did anything really useful or interesting, and it looks as if I never will. Sometimes I wish I'd never been born!"

He reiterates the despairing words, "I wish I'd never been born!" Like an answered prayer, they summon help from on high. A mysterious visitor shows George how important his life was to so many others by showing him how dreary things would have been had he never been born. He is given the gift to see how indispensable and, in fact, how wonderful his life really has been. Not to be born would have effaced all the good he had done, good that he somehow had forgotten about. George is spiritually reborn and returns to his loved ones with renewed appreciation and excitement.

Christmas, as we know, celebrates the birth of the Prince of Peace who comes into the world bearing a message of love and brotherhood. Peace and love, of course, are interconnected. The path to peace is through love. The particular form of love that Christmas emphasizes is love of neighbor. Dickens' *Christmas Carol* and the story of the *Grinch Who Almost Stole Christmas* are heartwarming yuletide tales because they chart the journeys of tepid souls who catch the Christmas spirit and become lovers of the neighbors.

The movie greatly amplifies and enriches Stern's short story. The tyrannical and parsimonious Mr. Potter, who is the very reincarnation of Ebenezer Scrooge, threatens Bedford Falls, a folksy town located somewhere in New York State. George Bailey—played by Jimmy Stewart, who delivers the most impassioned performance of his impressive career—gives Potter no quarter: "You sit around here and you spin your little webs and you think the whole world revolves around you and your money! Well, it doesn't Mr. Potter! In the whole vast configuration of things, I'd say you were nothing but a scurvy little spider!" Potter can neither own nor hire the intrepid George Bailey, so he decides to destroy him.

As the beleaguered George Bailey edges toward despair, it appears that Mr. Potter might succeed in his treacherous scheme, close the Bailey Building and Loan (on Christmas Eve) and turn Bedford Falls into a garish Babylon.

Thanks to the help of Clarence Oddbody, Angel Second Class, George is given a harrowing vision of what life in Bedford Falls would have been like had he never been born. "Strange, isn't it?" says the amiable Clarence, "Each man's life touches so many other lives, and when he isn't around he leaves an awful hole, doesn't he?" "You see," he tells George, who is now beginning to realize the significance of his life, "you've really had a wonderful life. Don't you see what a mistake it would be to throw it away?"

This endearing Christmas tale invites us to ask a larger question, "What would the present be like if Christ had never been born?" The question touches upon the very meaning of Christmas.

The great Medieval philosopher-theologian St. Thomas Aquinas once stated that "one difference between Christ and other men is this: they do not choose to be born, but He, the Lord and Maker of history, chose His time, His birthplace, and His mother." Christ chose to be born so that He could tell those who could not make the same choice, that life is indeed a great gift, one that we should cherish and enjoy. He came voluntarily into the world at Christmas to tell us to rejoice that we were born, and to provide the light we need so that we can value our life and share it with others. He chose to be born so that we could chose to be reborn. His physical birth was for our spiritual rebirth.

We are often tempted, like George Bailey, to measure our life in secular terms by the size of our bank account or the magnitude of our fame. When this happens, we lose sight of what is most important, the love we share with our neighbors and the life we enjoy with our friends. At such times, we need a light that helps us to see that our life is truly a great gift. Christmas is that light. And that light never ceases to shine.

Obedience

"The virtue of obedience is an exalted virtue," writes the distinguished Catholic philosopher, Jacques Maritain, "eminently reasonable; it is not in the least servile or blind, but requires on the contrary the greatest freedom of spirit and the strongest discernment."

Jean-Jacques Rousseau, another French philosopher, but not by any means as astute as Maritain, stated that the only people who are truly free are those who obey themselves and no one else. Rousseau did not trust any authority other than the self. But if he had been the least bit discerning, he would have recognized that the self is the most unreliable of all authorities. This is precisely why God commands us to obey Him. He is a more reliable authority than is any one of us. Though we may prefer to heed only our own will or to command others to obey our will, it is far more sensible and salutary for us to obey God's. "In his will is our peace," Dante writes, in his most celebrated phrase.

It is neither servile nor blind to obey God as well as those authorities who represent His Will. What is often servile and blind is obedience to one's ego, capitulation to impulse, acquiescence to the spur of the moment. Moreover, because we *choose* to obey or not to obey, obedience presupposes freedom.

Christ was obedient unto death, though His inclination was to be spared that "cup of suffering." No Christian can rightfully consider himself religious who does not recognize and live by the truth that obedience is a virtue.

One winter evening, in the year 1895, St. Thérèse of Lisieux was regaling some of her colleagues with stories about her childhood. One of the nuns, Sister Marie, turned to the Mother Superior and said: "Ah, Mother, what a pity we don't have this in writing: if you were to ask Sister Thérèse to write her childhood memories for you, what pleasure this would give us!" The response Mother Agnes of Jesus made was not a mere request, but a command. Addressing Thérèse, who was laughing at the moment because she thought her fellow sisters were teasing her, she said: "I order you to write down all your childhood memories." Surprised by this command, Thérèse humbly asked, "What can I write that you don't already know?" Nonetheless, she undertook the work out of obedience and apparently without reluctance, recognizing, as she stated, that her obedience to her Mother Superior was also obedience to Jesus.

Thérèse wrote her *Story of a Soul* (*l'Historie d'une âme*), and her love for obedience helped sustain her. "I am not writing to produce a literary work, but only through obedience . . . I must continue through obedience what I have begun through obedience," she wrote.

She finished her assignment with the words, "I go to Him with confidence and love." She was twenty-four and just a few months from death. According to novelist Frances Parkinson Keyes, "she had written one of the greatest works of all time." The person who did not try to write a literary work and understood that "true glory and the only royalty to be coveted lies in being unknown and esteemed as naught," had become, in spite of everything, a best selling and world famous author.

Story of a Soul has sold in the millions and has been translated into more than forty languages. Seventeen hundred churches have been named after St. Thérèse. Shortly after her death in 1897, reports of her miraculous intercession proliferated throughout the world. Pope Pius XI, who saw in her a "Word of God addressed to our times," canonized her in 1925. On October 19th 1997, the centennial of her passing, Pope John Paul II declared her a Doctor of the Church, one of only 33 saints to be so honored, and the third woman, after St. Teresa of Avila and St. Catherine of Sienna.

"He who lacks the virtue of obedience," wrote St. Teresa of Avila, "cannot be said to be a religious." God's loving Will remains unexpressed and unfelt wherever His intermediaries, we human beings, fail to obey Him. In retrospect, it appears that the Mother Superior's command to St. Thérèse to write her memoirs, was providential. It was providential in the strict sense of the term. Providence (coming from *pro* + *videre*) literally means to "see ahead." God can see the future. Our works can have a bearing on the future that we cannot see in the present, when we obediently place them in the hands of God who can see the future.

Toward the end of her life, Thérèse remarked, "I should like to die on the battlefield in defence of the Church." Through obedience one succeeds in this regard, as did the Little Flower, and so magnificently. Without obedience, however, too much emphasis is placed on the ego, on the "I." When this occurs, one does not stand in *defence*, but in *def"I"ance* of both God and the Church through which He endeavors to express His loving Will.

Piety

I am writing this article on Memorial Day, a time set aside for reflecting on the debt we owe to those who came before us and fought, struggled, and died in defending the values and privileges we often take for granted. Today is an occasion for thinking seriously and appreciatively about the virtue of piety.

The philosopher George Santayana once said that "A soul is but the last bubble of a long fermentation process in the world." "This consciousness," he went on to say, "that the human spirit is derived and responsible, that all its functions are heritages and trusts, involves a sentiment we may call piety."

Piety was a favorite virtue of Socrates. Far from considering himself a self-made man, the gadfly of Athens gave full credit for whatever civility he enjoyed to those who preceded him. Ralph Waldo Emerson, by contrast, America's head cheerleader for the man of self-reliance, spoke of "the sovereign individual, free, self-reliant, and alone in his greatness." Emerson's belief in the "greatness" of the individual is a dangerous illusion. It is a presumption that naturally leads to pride. In a very real sense, America's democratic spirit owes far more to Socrates than it does to Emerson. "Greatness" is never a purely individual accomplishment. Its roots are always in others and in times past. Sir Isaac Newton, with appropriate piety, saw himself as a mere "pygmy," but having the decisive advantage of standing on the shoulders of "giants." Albert Einstein stated, in rather moving prose, "A hundred times every day I remind myself that my inner and outer lives are based on the labors of other men, living and dead, and that I must exert myself in order to give in the same measure as I have received and am still receiving."

The great enemy of piety is individualism. Individualism is the illusion that we are somehow self-made, self-reliant, and self-sufficient. It is essentially an antisocial form of thinking that belongs to Nietzsche, Rousseau, Sartre, and Ayn Rand rather than to Socrates, St. Augustine, St. Thomas Aquinas, and the Founding Fathers of the American Constitution. The soul of individualism is unfettered choice. Abortion, for example, is presumed to be a private affair. Magically, as its advocates allege, it affects neither the child, its father, the family, or society. Yet every woman who has had an abortion was formed and brought into the world through the congress of parents and the labor of a mother. Pure individuality is sterile. No one begins his life *sui generis*. Our beginning coincides with a debt. Piety requires us to be grateful to those who begot us. It also evokes in us a duty to give what we have so that we can give to our descendents as our ancestors gave to us.

The basis of piety is the sober realization that we owe our existence and our substance to powers beyond ourselves. We are social, communal being. We are not islands; we are part of the main. The mere individual is a truncated being, shorn of both a heritage and a future. He is a fiction: Robinson Crusoe with a soul shivering for companionship. We are persons, possessors of unique abilities, but also inheritors of a social destiny.

"Individuality" is the result of a fall from grace. Adam and Eve behaved as persons until sin reduced them to individuals. As individuals, they began lusting after each other. The aprons of fig leaves they fashioned indicated that they were profoundly ashamed of their new identities as self-centered and self-absorbed individuals.

"Piety," said Cicero, "is justice towards the gods," and "the foundation of all virtues." By extension, piety is the just recognition of all we owe to our ancestors.

Plato was clearly one of the greatest philosophers who ever lived. Yet, he never wrote specifically about his own views. Though he wrote many lengthy and elaborate works in which he raised virtually every conceivable philosophical issue, he enshrined others, especially his beloved Socrates, as his mouthpieces. The explanation for this, as scholars have pointed out, is that Plato was living, as he was well aware, in a "post-war" society that had survived its own day of greatness. In recreating the mind of the principal philosopher of the fifth century B. C. and the circle in which he moved, he was expressing his duty in piety to Socrates, to the perished splendors of Athens, and to the notable Athenian family to which he belonged.

Memory recalls great moments past. A memorial enshrines them. A day of memorial is an occasion for collective reflection, tributes, and thanksgiving. Piety, by honoring what poured out from the past to become our own living substance, enlarges and enriches us. It disposes us to give thanks and to live in such a manner that we ourselves may one day become worthy objects for the thanks of others.

Queenliness

A jaundiced, dying man was brought to her on a stretcher. It was his last wish that he meet with her and be blessed by her gracious presence. "A lot of artists would not consent to meeting with a dying man," she said, "but I've been through enough in my life that I can relate to people very well. I'm not tough. I'm strong." In her case, *tough* describes a trait, *strong* depicts a virtue.

Who is this woman who is the object of a dying man's final request? And what has she lived through that gave her such strength?

She was born Eilleen Regina Edwards on August 28, 1965, in Windsor, Ontario. When she was just a toddler, her parents divorced. Her mother, Sharon, then took Eilleen and her two other daughters to live in Timmins. There, in this poor mining town about 250 miles north of Toronto, she married an Ojibwa Indian, a father of two boys. The new family of seven was reduced to six when Eilleen's older sister, Jill, left home at age fourteen. Eilleen thus became, in her words, "the older sister by default."

The family experienced excruciating poverty and the children learned painfully well what it means to be hungry. Eilleen would take a mustard sandwich to school with her for lunch. Her indigence made her feel embarrassed and isolated.

Tragedy struck when Eilleen was twenty-one. Her mother and step-father were killed in a head-on collision with a logging truck. The grim and numbing accident left Eilleen with custody of her three teenage siblings and the responsibility for raising them.

The Catholic poet, Thomas Traherne, asserted that "A Christian is an oak flourishing in winter." The adversity surrounding Eilleen's life made her strong. She abandoned her first name for the Ojibwa word *Shania* that means, "I'm on my way". She retained her step-father's surname, Twain. In this way, she took the name by which her millions of fans know her — Shania Twain.

She was indeed "on her way." Shania Twain has become one of the biggest-selling female singers in history. She is the first woman to have consecutive albums sell more than 10 million copies in the United States. She has won innumerable awards including Country Music Association's Entertainer of the Year and the 1999 Grammy Award. She was also named The Most Beautiful Canadian Woman of the Century.

Shania has not allowed her fame and wealth to obscure her past hardships or to ignore the hardships of others. Her compassion for others remains as strong as she remains strong as an individual. During some of her singing tours, she donates proceeds from each of her concerts to local charities that aid hungry children. "My goal," she states, "is to save kids the humiliation, the anguish of feeling inferior." Hers is the compassion that is worthy of the approbation of a Saint Augustine. The Bishop of Hippo wrote in his *Confessions*: "Although he that grieves with the grief-stricken is to be commended for his work of charity, yet the man who is fraternally compassionate would prefer to find nothing in others to need his compassion." There will be no need for compassion in Paradise.

Shania Twain enjoys a status that has much in common with royalty. She is a virtual "queen". Though not officially a member of royalty, she nonetheless carries her invisible crown with regal bearing. She exhibits the virtue of "queenliness." If kingliness is the virtue by which the king extends protection and fatherly love to all the members of his kingdom, queenliness is the collateral virtue by which the queen expresses compassion and caring concern for all the members of her queendom.

In helping to reverse the misfortunes of others, Shania is doing through music, what Charles Dickens did through his novels. Her identification with compassion for hungry children has not abated because, as she tells us, "I *was* that hungry kid."

Shania Twain's most personal song is "God Bless the Child," and she has pledged all royalties it earns to children's charities. The original title of the song was less catchy, though more instructive of its message: "Hallelujah, God Bless the Child Who Suffers."

The term *compassion* is commonly misinterpreted in our society to mean pity. The compassionate person, as the word indicates, suffers *with* the suffering person. And more than that, the compassionate person suffers *for* the suffering person. Pity causes a person to distance himself from the sufferer. There is no moral union between the one who pities and the object of his pity. Consequently, pity is inclined to end suffering by removing the sufferer. Compassion intuitively understands the redeeming value of suffering.

Marie Antoinette, born and raised with an aristocrat's unawareness of the plight of her indigent neighbors, suggested that they "eat cake" when informed that they had no bread. Compassion is formed in the real and heartrending experiences of deprivation. Shania Twain's adversity formed her compassion and her strength, and it is to her honor and credit that it retains priority in her heart far above all the trappings of her extraordinary success. Yet her immense success and great popularity have given her an opportunity to respond in the manner of a generous and compassionate queen. Queenliness may be a rare virtue, but it is as effective in its munificence as it is exalted in its comportment.

Resourcefulness

No distinguished American ever began his life under less promising circumstances. He was born to a slave woman on a farm near Diamond Grove, Missouri. His year of birth remains uncertain, but is estimated to be 1864. He was named George after his father. Because George senior died (in a farm accident on a plantation several miles away) before his son was born, the child had no surname.

When he was but an infant, nightriders, who trafficked in the slave market, kidnapped little George and his mother. Farmer Carver, his owner, sought at length to recover Mary and her son. He did succeed in regaining the child in exchange for a $300 racehorse. Unfortunately, he was never able to find the mother.

At first, Herr Carver and his wife believed that their retrieved child, found next to a tree, soaking wet and shaking with cold, was not going to live. When it appeared that he would survive, they feared that the persistent, hacking cough that choked his breath would leave him permanently speechless.

George took hold of life and did not lose his ability to speak. When he was barely ten years of age, he experienced what he would later describe as his "conversion." "God came into my heart one afternoon," he tells us, "while I was alone in the loft of our big barn." He remembers kneeling down at the time by a barrel of corn, and praying the best he could. It was an experience that nourished his unwavering faith for the rest of his life.

George, who took the surname of Moses Carver, who raised him, had to face difficulties other than his poverty, frail health, and orphaned status. Though he possessed an insatiable appetite for learning, he was often rebuffed because of his color. One instructor refused to teach him because he was black. Highland University denied him admission for the same reason. He was finally accepted at Simpson College in Indianola, Iowa. The school was named after a Methodist Bishop, Mathew Simpson, an Abolitionist and a lifetime friend of Abraham Lincoln. At Simpson he earned a bachelor's and a master's degree in agriculture.

His great ambition, even over-riding his dreams as a scientist, was to train and equip young black men and women so that they could become a more vital part of the American work force. He began to realize this ambition when Booker T. Washington invited him to join the faculty at Tuskegee Institute in Tuskegee, Alabama. Carver stayed there for 47 years and bequeathed his life savings of $33,000 to the school.

At the time of Carver's arrival, the Institute's agricultural department consisted of nothing more that a barn, a cow, and a few chickens. Ever resourceful and never discouraged, Carver instructed a small group of students on how to collect materials—pots, pans, tubes, wire, etc.—that could be used to construct laboratory equipment. "Throw nothing away. Everything can be used again!" These words were a virtual lifelong motto for the resourceful and ingenious George Washington Carver.

Carver persuaded southern farmers to diversify and rotate their crops by planting soil enriching peanuts and sweet potatoes instead of soul-exhausting cotton. His next task was to discover marketable uses for the superabundance of these new crops that were littering the fields. Here is where his resourcefulness proved to be of virtuoso caliber. From the peanut he made cheese, milk, coffee, flour, shampoo, axle grease, pickles, ink, dyes, soap, wood stains, and insulating board, to name but a few of his 300 products. The peanut quickly became a $200 million-a-year industry that not only rejuvenated the cotton fields, but also produced substantial revenues. From the sweet potato came vinegar, molasses, starch, breakfast food, tapioca, mucilage, crystallized ginger, synthetic rubber, and 100 additional products.

Carver was showered with many honors. The Roosevelt Medal, which he received in 1939, bore the citation, "For distinguished service in the field of science, to a scientist humbly seeking the guidance of God and a liberator of men of the white race, as well as the black." These words are most fitting inasmuch as they underscore his faith in God and his service to mankind. Carver's resourcefulness was inseparable from his faith in God's Providence. God loves to hide his secrets; humans love to discover them. George Washington Carver was both a seeker and a finder.

At the time of his death, in 1943, eighteen schools were named in his honor. Carver, himself, would have deflected the attention to God, who had not forsaken, toward the end of the Civil War, a child who began his sojourn on earth orphaned, enslaved, destitute, abandoned, and sick. God's own resourcefulness will not be outdone.

Simplicity of Heart

The Book of Wisdom opens by enjoining us to "Love virtue" and to seek the Lord "in simplicity of heart." It advises us not to be so untrusting as to think that God could deceive us. And it counsels us not to be so foolish as to think we can outwit Him. Therefore, it invites us to open our hearts to God and be united with Him in the purity of a heart-to-heart relationship.

Simplicity of heart is indispensable in approaching God. It is also indispensable in establishing any real friendship. Indeed, friendship is a heart-to-heart relationship, the embodiment of that conversation between hearts that John Henry Newman honored when he became Cardinal by inscribing the words *"Cor ad cor loquitur"* on his shield.

Simplicity of heart allows us to be who we are in our relationships with others. It represents a certain genuineness in speech, dress, and behavior. The opposite of simplicity, in this sense, is *duplicity*. We are one in our being. But we are often divided. This happens when we separate the being we are from the being we would like to be. The fashion industry thrives on this division by encouraging us to adopt an alien image of ourselves. It is this alien image that we often feel obliged to present to the world. And we can become so absorbed by this fictitious image, that we lose touch with who we really are.

Another and more trenchant word for "duplicity" is *phoniness*. No one admires a phony, yet people spend billions of dollars a year to be exactly that. Even if the particularly kind of phoniness we display happens to be "in style," it is nonetheless phony.

The world of glamour, it is often said, is only skin deep. As such, it does not reach deep enough to include the heart. We find ourselves "putting on the Ritz," "trying to make an impression," "showing off," being "hip," "trendy," "with it," and "up-to-date." But these synthetic approaches can alienate the heart. When this occurs, we begin to hunger for "simplicity of the heart," the virtue that transcends fashion and is never out-of-date. Simplicity of the heart is the virtue that allows us to reveal to another what is in our hearts. In this regard, it is the virtue of the eternal child. Children want to tell their parents and their siblings what is in their hearts. They are not yet interested in being devious, cunning, or deceitful. They are not trying to impress anyone. They want to know where they came from, whether they are loved, who made the stars, and what will the future bring. Their hearts vibrate with wonder.

It is most important that parents honor and preserve the simplicity of heart that is an innate quality in their children. This means that mom and dad must make some effort to reawaken their own simplicity of heart.

The great American novelist, Nathaniel Hawthorne, by all accounts, was a splendid father. His daughter Rose, who later became Mother Alphonsa, writes engagingly about moments of grace she shared with him when she was a young girl. "To play a simple game of stones on one of the grey benches in the late afternoon sunshine with him for my courteous opponent, was to feel my eyes, lips, hands, all my being, glowing with the fullness of human happiness."

A good parent understands how much he can learn from his children. Children speak, primarily because they are born with a need to disclose what is in their hearts. In this sense, they have something in common with Solomon. It is as if they had read, but only dimly remembered, the opening lines of his *Book of Wisdom*. The image of Nathaniel Hawthorne taking time off from work on *The Blithedale Romance* or *Tanglewood Tales* or *The Marble Faun* to sit with his daughter and play a simple game of stones, is a wonderful image of heart-speaking-to-heart, without the distraction or the adulteration of ulterior motives. It is the simplicity of one heart resonating with the simplicity of another. "Selfish intentions divorce from God," warns Solomon. Unselfish openness allows love and friendship to form and flourish.

Parents, through their love for their children, will revive their own simplicity of the heart. This is their children's gift to them. The parents' corresponding gift to their children will be prudence, caution, and discernment. We do not want to wear our hearts on our sleeves, and we have been advised not to "cast our pearls before swine." Simplicity of heart is a virtue that does not need to be expressed at every opportunity. One must be circumspect. But it is a virtue that is indispensable for prayer and essential to the formation of any honest friendship.

Our age, which promotes unremittingly the synthetic, artificial look, neither appreciates nor encourages simplicity of heart. There is simply no money to be made from human beings getting in touch with their own hearts. Yet, it is a virtue we all long for and greatly admire when we see it in others. It is a certain genuineness that children bring into the world that calls their parents back to their own simplicity. The family, then, has the holy obligation to revitalize simplicity of the heart in a world that is numbing itself to death by trying to be fashionable.

Temperance

Shakespeare could not have achieved pre-eminence as a writer solely on the basis of his style, inimitable as it is. He needed a moral vision in order to imbue his characters with a human credibility that would continue to engage and inspire his audiences and readers throughout the ages. Moreover, in giving form to the enduring nature of the human being, that moral vision had to transcend the politics and trends of his time. The distinguished Harvard historian, Arthur Schlesinger, Jr., ranks Shakespeare as being the world's single most influential thinker over the past 1,000 years.

Shakespeare knew, therefore, that virtue is noble and vice is base, that love is lasting and lust is ephemeral. He did not need to moralize, exactly, but his words, enunciated by his characters in response to their dramatic situations, made it unmistakable that good is desirous, whereas evil is despicable. "There's a divinity that shapes our ends, Rough-hew them how we will" (*Hamlet,* Act v, sc.2, l.10).

Shakespeare wrote a great deal about love, and often contrasted it with its deadly opposite, lust. He expressed considerable wisdom with regard to that particular species of temperance that is applied to human sexuality and is known as chastity. In *The Tempest* (Act iv, sc.1, 1.56), Prospero explains why Ferdinand's love must be chaste:

> . . . take my daughter: but
> If thou dost break her virgin-knot before
> All sanctimonious ceremonies may
> With full and holy rite be minister'd
> No sweet aspersion shall the heavens let fall
> To make this contract grow; but barren hate,

Sour-eyed disdain and discord shall bestrew
The union of your bed with weeds so loathly
That you shall hate it both . . .

Ferdinand then professes his undying love for Prospero's daughter, Miranda. His words convince his future father-in-law that the love he has for Miranda is bound so firmly to honor that there is no possibility that it could ever provide an entrance point for lust. Ferdinand declares that his love for his bride-to-be—as person, wife, and mother—is chaste and a most secure safeguard against any temptation that might confront him.

As I hope
For quiet days, fair issue and long life,
With such love as 'tis now, the murkiest den,
The most opportune place, the strong'st suggestion
Our worse genius can, shall never melt
Mine honour into lust, to take away
The edge of that day's celebration
When I shall think, or Phoebus' steeds are founder'd
Or Night kept chain'd below.

Virtue is a fortress against vice. Temperance is a fortress against dissipation. Chastity excludes lust. Honor binds love in the present to love in the future. Since it lives and thrives on the plane of the eternal, it rejoices in making vows, in professing commitment. Ferdinand's pledge to Miranda is made with such confidence that it seems to him that no power including Satan himself (symbolized by "our worse genius") could ever dissolve his love into lust.

Chastity is problematic in the contemporary world because love and honor are often mistaken for their adversaries. Love is therefore confused with lust, while honor is confused with feeling sincere. Both lust and feeling sincere are transitory. Instead of making sense of chastity, they make a mockery of it.

We might imagine a contemporary anti-Ferdinand who is tuned in to the current trends, proffering his feelings toward

Miranda in anticipation of their impending marriage. He would hedge his bets, put the right "spin" on his words, and convince himself that he far nobler than he really is. But his lack of love would be transparent.

As long as
My inconstant powers don't fail me,
I mean to honour her and show my due commitment
In a thousand diverse ways;
Yet, forged as I am to mortal flesh,
To pledge too much is most intemperate.

As Nature in her own and unexpected ways
Chills early Spring, sends warming breeze into the
Heart of Winter,
My vows will also prove as variable.
Respecting this hard truth, one I did not design,
I promise what I can - my impassioned hope that Fate
Will marry faithful hearts in bliss.

Hearing such a declaration, Prospero would not have responded, as he did in the play, with the words, "Fairly spoke. Sit, then, and talk with her; she is thine own." He would have been enraged by the suitor's Machiavellian subterfuge.

Consider Shakespeare's expansive poem, *Venus and Adonis*, which is his first formally published work and the apparently the very first of all his creative works (if we may so interpret his calling it "the first heir of my invention"). In line 799, Adonis expatiates on the evident differences between love and lust. He seems to be appealing to what we already know about these two opposites. Those who have experienced both love and lust, know, without fear of error, that love is incomparably more gratifying.

Love comforteth like sunshine after rain,
But lust's effect is tempest after sun;
Love's gentle spring doth always fresh remain,

Lust's winter comes ere summer half be done:
Love surfeits not. Lust like a glutton dies;
Love is all truth, Lust full of forged lies.

Again, we may wonder how a contemporary anti-
Shakespeare would phrase his thoughts so that *lust* appears to
be more honest, natural, immediate, and plausible than *love*.
The trendy spin-meister can make anything seem to be anything he wants it to be.

Lust is Nature's answer for my pain
For something quick and earthly must be done;
Love applies its remedy in vain,
Impractical as shackling the sun;
Lust is here and now, before our eyes,
While love has its abode beyond the skies.

To the modern mind, love is *idealistic*, whereas lust is *practical*. But the modern mind is anything but morally practical. By
dismissing ideals that bring fulfillment to life, it does not indicate that it prefers realism to idealism, but in fact, convenience
to authenticity. An ideal, such as love, that answers the
profoundest needs in the human being, is by no means unrealistic. What is essentially unrealistic is the notion that we can find
meaning and fulfillment through lust.

Shakespeare's incomparable synthesis of style and substance, however, constitutes an argument of its own. We read
Shakespeare or listen to his words articulated from the stage
and they ring true. We follow with both our minds and hearts.
He involves all of who we are. Without preaching, he presents
chastity not only as attractive, but also as irrefutable. How could
we argue against the gracious words of Katharine of Aragon in
Henry VIII? "When I am dead . . . strew me over with maiden
flowers, that all the world may know I was a chaste wife to my
grave" (Act iv, sc. 2, l. 170). And yet Shakespeare is wise enough

to remind us that we often choose, we fallible mortals, that
which is both unwise and counterproductive:

The expense of spirit in a waste of shame
Is lust in action; and till action, lust
Is perjured, murderous, bloody, full of blame,
Savage, extreme, rude, cruel, not to trust;
Enjoyed no sooner, but despised straight;
Past reason hunted; and no sooner had,
Past reason hated, as a swallowed bait,
On purpose laid to make the taker mad:
Mad in pursuit, and in possession so;
Had, having, and in quest to have, extreme;
A bliss in proof, and proved, a very woe;
Before, a joy proposed; behind, a dream.
All this the world well knows; yet none knows well
To shun the heaven that leads men to this hell. (*Sonnet*
cxxxix)

Hamlet's advice to actors can also be applied to the sphere
of sexual morality: ". . . in the very torrent, tempest, and, as I
may say, whirlwind of your passion, you must acquire and beget
a temperance that may give it smoothness" (*Hamlet,* Act II, sc.
1, l. 7).

It is not so much that chastity, temperance applied to sexuality, is not plausible or realistic. The problem is with us, that
we are often weak and foolish. Why have we not learned by
now, after all these centuries and all the patent and embarrassing sexual indiscretions human beings have committed, that the
lustful choice of a transitory pleasure brings shame, regret, and
punishment?

Sigmund Freud once commented that in human beings,
there is an inveterate tendency to "over-estimate the unattained
sexual object." His language, needless to say, is far less elegant
and poetic than Shakespeare's. Yet the Bard and the Austrian
psychoanalyst have much in common on this point. We tend to

idealize sex and depreciate love. When we are betrayed, once again, by our lust, we experience shame and regret. But do we ever learn? The cynical expressions, "chaste is waste" and "vice is nice" need to be replaced by more realistic expressions, such as "lechery is treachery" or "cupidity is stupidity."

Chastity is eminently realistic. It does not falsely idealize the other. It is inseparable from love and therefore riveted to the good of the other. In his book, *Christ in Shakespeare*, George H. Morrison says, with the Bard in mind: "We never see rightly till we love . . . Only when we love do we discover the hidden treasures of personality. And Shakespeare is a far-off follower of Him who loved, and saw what no one had ever seen before."

According to an ancient maxim, *Ubi amor, ibi oculus* (Where there is love, there is knowledge). Love allows us entrance into the reality of the other person. Chastity is the virtue that allows us to love the other realistically on a sexual level, that is, the fundamental good of the other person. As Shakespeare teaches, chastity is the combination of love and honor that allows us to serve the beloved through thick and thin. It is a promise and a commitment; but it is also a capacity and a power. The better we love and the more we know about honor, the easier it will be for us to be chaste.

Unpretentiousness

Doris Kearns Goodwin lives in Concord, Massachusetts, not far from the Old North Bridge. It was from that "rude" construction, in Ralph Waldo Emerson's deathless words, that "the embattled farmers stood, / And fired the shot heard round the world." Goodwin is a noted historian whose books on the Fitzgeralds and the Kennedys, Lyndon Johnson, and Franklin D. Roosevelt have brought her great acclaim, with the latter, *No Ordinary Time*, earning her a Pulitzer Prize.

Yet, when she takes visitors to that historic site, she thinks not of the epic moment which launched the American revolution, but Bobby Thomson's shot into the left field seats at the Polo Grounds that ended the Dodgers pennant hopes in 1951.

Her memoir, *Wait Till Next Year* (1997), which made the *New York Times* "Best-Seller List," reveals the eternal child in her, the one whose formative years paralleled the career of her idol, Jackie Robinson. Baseball was her passion long before she knew anything about the impact that American presidents have had on modern history. And it has remained a passion with her. Ms. Goodwin enjoys the peculiar distinction of being the first woman ever to enter the locker room of the Boston Red Sox.

While preparing for Confirmation, as she tells us in her memoir, a youthful and impressionable Doris Kearns won a Catholic Catechism contest. Her prize, which she had sought with uncommon diligence, was a St. Christopher medal that had been blessed by the Pope.

She had immediate and important plans for her newly acquired trophy. It was to cure the Brooklyn Dodgers first baseman, Gil Hodges, of a prolonged batting slump. "If St. Christopher could protect travelers," thought the enterprising Miss Kearns, "perhaps he could ensure the safe passage of Gil

Hodges around the bases." Her logic may have been faulty, but her heart was in the right place.

The time was propitious. The slumping Mr. Hodges was soon appearing at Wolf's Sport Shop on nearby Sunrise Highway to sign autographs. Her plan was to present him with her holy icon and thereby break him out of his hitting drought. She finagled her mother into driving her to the scene, and after waiting in line until she was face-to-face with her wilting hero, handed him her unusual bromide along with a carefully rehearsed monologue: "This medal has been blessed by the Pope and I had won it in a catechism contest when I knew the seventh deadly sin was gluttony, and I thought St. Christopher would watch over [your] swing so that [you] could return home safely each time [you] went to bat and would make me feel good and would make Dodger fans all over the world feel great."

She concluded her rambling, but charming disquisition amidst the good-natured laughter from others standing around her. But Mr. Hodges responded with solemnity and graciousness. He confided that he, too, once had a St. Christopher medal blessed by the Pope. But he had seen fit to give it to his father, a coal-miner in Indiana. Mr. Hodges, senior, had broken his back, lost an eye, and severed three toes in a series of mining accidents. The towering first baseman thought that his dad needed the medal more than he did. He was thrilled, he said, to receive a medal of his own. Then, he reached out in a gesture of gratitude and enveloped the delicate hand of Miss Kearns in a massive palm that was several times the size of her own. Indeed, his Dodger teammates joked that his hands were so large that he didn't need a glove. He was the perfection of unpretentiousness. Miraculously (or otherwise), after accepting his amulet, Hodges regained his batting eye virtually overnight.

Being pretentious is making claim to being important. It is the opposite of being modest and unassuming. Hodges could very well have laid claim to a certain measure of importance. He played in the major leagues for 18 years. And after a brief retirement, managed the "Miracle Mets" to their 1969 World

Championship. He hit 20 or more home runs for 11 consecutive seasons and batted in more than 100 runs for 7 straight years. He established a National League record with 14 career grand slams, hit 4 round trippers in one game, and 3 times won the Gold Glove award for his slick fielding at first base. And he drove in the game's only two runs when the "Bums" from Flatbush defeated the hated Yankees in the deciding game of the 1955 World Series to give Dodger fans their only World Series Championship. But it was enough that he played for the Brooklyn Dodgers to justify, in the eyes of his fans who had lined up that day for his autograph, his acting "important."

To his credit, however, he did not act as if he were important. For the moment he was not a major league ballplayer. He was a son who revered his dad, and a host who was beguiled by a charming young girl who risked embarrassing herself before a lineup of strangers.

Gilbert Raymond Hodges died of a heart attack in 1972, two days before his 48th birthday. His burial site is marked by a simple gravestone in Holy Cross Cemetery in Brooklyn, NY. Death provides a perspective in which the more important features of a person's life seem to be truly more important. Hodges has not as yet been inducted into the Hall of Fame, though many of his supporters claim that he is one of the best ballplayers of all time who has not been enshrined in that special pantheon. Perhaps Dodger catcher Roy Campanella had things in the right perspective when he said of his teammate: "Gil Hodges is a hall of fame man." Hodges' character, his integrity, and his charming unpretentiousness have not gone unnoticed. The fans noticed, as did his teammates. Dodger pitcher Clem Labine testified: "Gil Hodges was the only player I can remember whom the fans never, I mean never booed." And Dodger shortstop Pee Wee Reese remarked: "If you had a son, it would be a great thing to have him grow up to be just like Gil Hodges."

There can be little doubt that what most impressed Miss Kearns that day at Wolf's Sport Shop, as well as her readers many years later, was not tales of Mr. Hodges' prowess at the plate, but his unpretentiousness among people. Unpretentiousness is the virtue that allows one to discover what is really important in another, not in the midst of fanfare, but in the silent communication between two souls. There is a light that shines more brightly than stardom because it shines from the heart. Doris Kearns felt the warmth from that light when she was a young girl, and it has continued to glow in her own heart ever since.

Veracity

Truth can be most inconvenient and unattractive to anyone who has grown accustomed to a comfortable myth. The complacent individual who attaches himself to a myth, like the barnacle that fixes itself to the side of a ship, is most reluctant to dissolve an alliance that has proved to be both congenial and undemanding. Love for truth, which veracity presupposes, is not a commonplace disposition of the soul. It requires an uncommon willingness to submit to something that is wholly outside the ego. And it often exacts a price. G. K. Chesterton once referred to pride as "the falsification of fact by the introduction of self." Veracity requires a humility pure enough that it seeks nothing of the self and everything of the other. It also requires dedication and courage, and a strong affection for contemplation. "Veracity," write Dietrich and Alice von Hildebrand, "is, like reverence, fidelity, or constancy and the awareness of responsibility, a basis of our whole moral life . . . Veracity is the basis for all true community life, for every relationship of person to person, for every true love, for every profession, for true knowledge, for self-education, and for the relationship of men to God."

Doctors Meyer Friedman and Gerald W. Friedland, authors of *Medicine's 10 Greatest Discoveries* (Yale University Press, 1998), both came to the conclusion, independently of each other, that the greatest discovery in the history of medicine was William Harvey's discovery in 1628 of the circulatory system.

Harvey was adroit enough to realize that the presentation of such a jarring truth would be met with great resistance, if not strong ridicule. Most cautiously and respectfully, he prepared his readers for his startling revelation by warning them, after seven carefully worded chapters that led up to his conclusion, that his next words would be "of so novel and unheard-of character, that I not only fear injury to myself from the envy of a few, but I tremble lest I have mankind at large for my enemies." And then he announced: *I began to think whether there might be a motion, as it were, in a circle.* Despite his great care, in both his science and his phrasing, Harvey was bitterly maligned by his European contemporaries. The great anatomist was merely suggesting that blood flowed from the heart through arteries and back to that same organ through veins in a circular fashion ("Which motion we may be allowed to call *circular*").

What we now embrace as a truism Harvey introduced with great (and justifiable) trepidation. We boast rather easily of seeking the truth. But when we confront it, stripped of all mythology, it often seems unrecognizable and alien to us. We prefer our accustomed illusions. Though they are illusions, they at least have the comforting attraction of being familiar and recognizable.

Harvey published approximately 200 copies of *Exertatio anatomica de motu cordis et sanguinis in animalibus* (An anatomical treatise on the motion of the heart and blood in animals) of which 53 are believed extant. It is widely regarded as the most important book ever published in the field of medicine.

When it comes to seeing truth, we have 20-20 hindsight, but our present-sight is not nearly as acute. We learn of the mistakes and the insights of our predecessors long before, indeed, if we ever, learn of our own. History should teach us humility, though we often blindly assume that we will not repeat the mistakes of our predecessors.

Another great hematologist, lover of truth, and a man of veracity who is worthy of attention, is Charles Richard Drew. He was a pioneer in preserving blood. He made the breakthrough discovery that blood plasma, which could be preserved for a long period of time, could replace whole blood, which deteriorated after a few days in storage. As a scientist who stood fast by truth, he understood that "blood is blood" and that its nature is entirely extrinsic to a person's race or skin color. Therefore, he knew that there is no scientific basis for segregating blood supplies in hospitals according to race, and no scientific reason to oppose the transfusing of blood from a white person to a black, or *vice versa.*

Charles Richard Drew was born in 1904 in a black neighborhood in the so-called Foggy Bottom area of Washington, D. C. He first imagined himself becoming a doctor at age 15 when he watched helplessly as his sister died of tuberculosis. He attended Amherst College, a black student within a nearly exclusive white student body. There, he excelled at sports, being captain of the track team and making All-American as quarterback of the football squad. He needed money after graduation and taught biology and chemistry at Morgan State College in Baltimore, where he also served as the school's athletic director.

In 1928 he entered the McGill University Medical School in Montreal. It was there that he became interested in blood research. He received his Master of Surgery and Doctor of Medicine Degrees from McGill in 1933. Seven years later, and after a brief stint of teaching at Howard University Medical School, he became the first black to receive the degree of Doctor of Science in Medicine from Columbia University. His doctoral thesis at Columbia, "Banked Blood," was based on an exhaustive study of blood preservation techniques. He discovered a way of separating and storing blood plasma to the point where it could become a practical reality.

The technique he developed for the long-term preservation of blood catapulted him onto the world stage. He was called upon to serve as a full-time Medical Director of the "Blood for Britain" project, supervising the successful collection of 14,000 pints of vital plasma for the British. In February 1941, he was appointed Director of the first American Red Cross Blood Bank, in charge of blood for use by the Unites States Army and Navy.

Drew's life took a dramatic turn later that year when the War department sent out a directive stating that blood taken from White donors should be segregated from blood taken from Black donors. He called a press conference to point out the simple, scientifically established truth that blood from Whites and Blacks is indistinguishable. Amidst, widespread controversy, Dr. Drew sharply criticized the directive and resigned his post. He returned to Howard University where he taught until his untimely death in 1950, two months before his 46th birthday.

On his way to a medical conference in Tuskegee, Alabama, the car in which Charles Richard Drew and three other physicians were traveling struck a soft shoulder of the road and overturned. The steering wheel crushed Drew's chest; he suffered a multitude of injuries and died within an hour of the accident.

The circumstances of this tragic event became an occasion for spreading a myth about his demise, ironically, the kind of distortion of the facts that Drew himself had tirelessly and valiantly opposed throughout his life.

According to the myth, Drew's life may have been saved by means of a blood transfusion, but the nearby "White" hospitals, because of their blood segregation policy, refused to provide him with the life-saving serum that he needed. In this way, Drew was allegedly a victim of the very bigotry that he had vigorously denounced.

Charles E. Wynes' biography of Charles Richard Drew—*Charles Richard Drew: the Man and the Myth* (University of Illinois Press, 1988)—sets the record straight. He quotes the other doctors who had accompanied Drew on that fateful ride. They, as well as a former student of Drew who happened to be at the hospital that night—all of whom being black—testified that the treatment Dr. Drew received was perfectly adequate. Drew's own wife concurred in this evaluation. Drew did, as a matter of fact, receive "at least one blood transfusion."

Dr. Ford, one of the black physicians who was in the accident with Drew, stated: "Doctor Drew's cause of death was that of a broken neck and complete blockage of the blood flow back to the heart. Immediately following the accident in which he was half thrown out of the car, and actually crushed to death by the car as it turned over a second time, the doctors who were able to, got out of the car quickly and came to Doctor Drew's rescue, but it was of no avail because even at that time, it was quite obvious that his chances of surviving were nil."

For some, the myth of Drew's death seems more appealing than what actually took place. Prejudice dies hard. We are often reluctant to see, understand, and accept the truth, especially when it stands in conflict with a myth that has achieved the status of being politically correct.

Medical history from Harvey to Drew is replete with instances in which the myth is given priority over the truth. The best way to honor an honorable man is to honor what he honored. We honor the likes of Harvey, Drew, and others by committing ourselves more fervently to a love for truth and its consequent courage and veracity.

The reluctance to be enthused about truth, needless to say, is not confined to medicine (although the reluctance to acknowledge the truth of the unborn human, so common among present-day medical personnel, is most disturbing). The poet A. E. Housman once said that our desire for truth is the "faintest" of all our passions. Philosophy professor Allan Bloom lamented how today's students are systematically misled into thinking that truth cannot be attained. The author of *The Closing of the American Mind* found it extremely frustrating in trying to lead his students out of Plato's cave and into the light of truth: "The *Republic's* story of man in the cave still exercises some of its old magic, but it now encounters a fresh obstacle, for the meaning of the story is that truth is substituted for myth. Today's students are taught that no such substitution is possible" (*Crisis*, April 1993, p. 25).

"You will learn the truth and the truth shall make you free" (Jn 8:32). But we must first cultivate a love for truth. We talk glibly of freedom, but then resist setting foot on the path of truth that leads to freedom. We like the end but not the means, the fruit but not the labor. We also speak glibly about justice, and then disdain the path of truth that leads to its fruitful vineyard.

Veracity is a great virtue. And because it is a virtue, it is not given to us as our birthright. It must be achieved. We must have the faith to believe that whatever the truth is, it will be, in the final analysis, consonant with the good, and productive of freedom.

The Charles R. Drew University of Medicine and Science in Los Angeles, a U. S. postage stamp, and numerous medical facilities honor a man whose love for truth and resistance to prejudice saved innumerable lives, both white and black. Those who honor him, may applaud his accomplishments. But they would honor him more by imitating his veracity (as well as his tenacity). It is difficult to *undiscover* something that is already discovered. Past discoveries will remain with us. But love for truth puts us in a position to make new discoveries. We profit from the achievements of others, but it is through imitating their love for truth, courage, and veracity, that we ourselves can benefit posterity.

Wisdom

Life is certainly confusing; especially if you have no principles to give it coherence, direction, and meaning. Without principles we become mere spectators to a life that we can neither comprehend nor enjoy. Shakespeare once described such an existence as a "tale told by an idiot, full of sound and fury, signifying nothing." It belongs to the province of wisdom, as the sages of the past have declared, to put things in their proper order (*Sapientis est ordinare*). Yet wisdom in our age has been blurred and obscured by the present information glut. Thus the lamentation of T. S. Eliot: "Where is the wisdom we have lost in knowledge? Where is the knowledge we have lost in information?" Where is the wisdom, we might also ask, we have lost in our educational institutions?

I have spent a significant part of my life trying to convince students in my ethics classes (I refrain from identifying them as "ethics students") of the indispensable value of good moral principles. Teaching, as someone once said, is the art of putting abstract ideas into concrete heads. I would prefer to think of it as awakening my students to reality. My pupils, in general, like concreteness. For them, it is the very synonym of reality. It is "abstractness" (sometimes known as "philosophy") that they distrust. And our materialistic world has convinced so many of them, without their permission or understanding, that abstractions are not part of the real world. Hence the elusiveness of wisdom.

So I began one class by pointing out how *practical* principles are. "Imagine," I suggested, "the impracticality of a telephone directory that lists the names of people and their corresponding phone numbers in random order. Is not the principle of alphabetical order, indeed, most practical?" One student pondered what I had said and then offered an objection: "I organize *my* personal telephone book according to frequency of use." He did not recognize that he was utilizing a principle, though a very odd one that would require incessant updating. But it was *his* principle and he felt that he had successfully prevented me from "imposing" one of "mine" on his free spirit.

On another occasion, and after my initial class one fine fall evening, a rather anxious student accompanied me out to the parking lot explaining to me how at sea I was with regard to my grasp of moral principles. He confessed having done something during the summer that left him with a deep and painful sense of regret. His single life principle was "never experience regret." He rejected "do *good* and avoid *evil*." He dismissed both these notions as being excessively vague. Being an existentialist of sorts, he, too, was primarily interested in concreteness, particularly his own feelings.

I tried, without success, to explain to him that "not experiencing regret" is not an object of choice, either for him or for anyone else. If it were, everyone would choose it, and no one would ever experience regret. "Do good," I proposed, "and you will experience peace, the natural preventative of regret. Neither happiness nor 'not feeling regret' is an object of choice. Each is a consequence of our choosing or not choosing something else. It is precisely that 'something else' that should occupy our attention." Wisdom always appears in a paradoxical form. This helps to explain why it is so rare.

Now standing next to my car, I noticed how the smoke my student was exhaling obscured his features. There will be a time, I thought to myself, when he will come to regret his involvement with the wicked weed. He was already scheduling his date with regret. My words fell on deaf ears. He insisted on being *my* teacher. After all, he had been taught by experience itself. He was the one who was realistic and practical. "Regret is painful. Don't experience it!" That's all there is to it. Life is really quite simple. But he was not aware of the dangers inherent in his own narcissism. If there is one way to insure the arrival of regret, it is to place your private interests above those of everyone else's.

I saw little of this student until the day before the end of the term. He came into my office in a desperate mood. He had not attended any more of my classes and asked if I could give him my notes so he could study for the final exam. I explained that, unfortunately, I had no such notes to give him and suggested that he obtain them from another student. He confessed, forlornly, that he did not know anyone in the class. Regret was weighing heavily on my poor student. I was careful not to mention the word. He needed a miracle, not a sermon.

A teacher wants his students to learn in the classroom, not in the school of hard knocks that can leave them hopeless and defeated. What would G. K. Chesterton have said to my distressed student? He had a genius for making philosophy so irresistible to common sense that it provoked not opposition, but enlightened laughter. How would he, who had mastered the art of bringing abstract principles to life by marrying them to the right image and phrase, have handled the matter?

Philosophers are *pedagogues*, a word that has an interesting association with walking. In *What's Wrong with the World?* Chesterton refers to a nearly forgotten notion that is "most nearly paralleled by the principle of the second wind in walking." "The principle is this," as he explains: "That in everything worth having, even in every pleasure, there is a point of pain or tedium that must be survived so that the pleasure may revive and endure." The pleasure of learning comes only after the inconvenience of studying. The joy of victory comes only after the boredom of training. The pride of graduation comes only after the pain of perseverance. But neither learning, victory, nor graduation could eventuate unless we survived the inevitable moments of inconvenience, boredom, and pain. "In everything on this earth that is worth doing, there is a stage when no one would do it, except for necessity or honor."

Chesterton's "principle of the second wind" flows from a wise soul. Life is difficult because we find ourselves at the center of divergent forces. There is the pull toward our convenience and the pull in the opposite direction toward the good of others. How much of one should there be, and how much of the other? Wisdom cannot be reduced to a simplistic bromide, such as "avoid regret." It offers enlightenment when it represents a vision that transcends both simplicities and polarities. This is the essence of wisdom. The success of teaching is realized only after surviving the ordeal and frustration that both patience and commitment require. We learn wisdom slowly. Wisdom is paradoxical and transcendent. It requires honor, fidelity, and an abiding love that will never grow stale.

Xuberance

(E)xuberance is a ripe and resplendent word. *Uber* in Latin refers to the female breast. Etymologically, an exuberant person is one who has greatly benefited from the abundant flow of life and love he has received from his mother. Oliver Wendell Holmes was being justifiably exuberant in his praise of breast feeding, not to mention amusing, when he said that "a pair of substantial mammary glands has the advantage over the two hemispheres of the most learned professor's brain in the art of compounding a nutritious fluid for infants."

In terms of its common usage, "exuberance" conveys the qualities of being fertile and filled. Applied to a particular human being, it suggests a superabundance of *joie de vivre*. Exuberance, therefore, is redolent with incarnational significance and hence a very good Christian term. It is vital, bodily, and spiritual all at the same time. Christians should be exuberant. Their joy should be evident. Man fully alive is the glory of God.

Let us turn the pages of history to the year 1232 (or thereabouts) when there came into the world a man destined to be one of the most exuberant personalities in the annals of Christendom. His name is Ramón Llull, and his birthplace is the Mediterranean island of Majorca.

Llull's father, a wealthy merchant from Barcelona, settled on Majorca with James I of Aragon the year after the king had conquered the island from the Moors. In effect, Llull was a child of Muslim-Christian inheritance. He was raised and educated at Court, and was eventually appointed a seneschal (a steward in charge of the royal palace) to the young James II. Traditional accounts tell colorful stories of Llull, especially in his role as a troubadour.

Llull was once smitten by a young unmarried woman. True

to his romantic and flamboyant nature, he rode his horse into the center of the church, where she was praying during a worship service, in order to impress her with his love. She had her duenna arrange an assignation, and, when alone with Llull, confessed her own affection for him. In a most dramatic gesture, she then exposed that portion of her body that was already ravaged by cancer. She had only a few weeks to live. The impact on Llull was staggering and left him, for some time, in a state of emotional shock.

Sometime thereafter, and having been inspired by a Franciscan sermon, Llull renounced his life at court and dispossessed himself of all his worldly goods. He made pilgrimages to Rocamadour, to Santiago de Compostela, and to other shrines, and subsequently joined the Franciscan order. During the years 1263 or 1264, Llull had repeated visions of Christ crucified. It was as a consequence of these mystical experiences that he conceived the idea that he had been chosen to convert Islam to Christianity. In order to take the first step in achieving this grandiose project, he needed to learn Arabic. To this end, he secured the services of an Arab slave to teach him the language. When this task was accomplished, and Llull had some command of the slave's mother tongue, he attempted to convert his teacher to Christianity. Llull failed miserably, however. In his extreme frustration, whatever the particulars of the circumstance may have been, Llull flew into a rage and killed his slave. His remorse over such an impetuous and violent act caused so profound a remorse in him that he vowed that from that moment on, he would live by only one rule: "He who loves not lives not." Forevermore, he abandoned the sword to live by love and to persuade by logic.

Llull's life is an icon of exuberance and indefatigability. His love for the Church and his enthusiasm for converting Muslims never diminished. On the academic side, his accomplishments were astonishing. He wrote 228 books on almost every important topic of his age. He wrote on philosophy, geometry, astronomy, physics, chemistry, anthropology, law, statecraft, navigation, horsemanship, and warfare. He perfected the astrolabe, anticipated problems in thermo-dynamics, and held strong to the position that there was a great continent on the other side of the world. He was also, apart from being a prolific logician, a very good poet, and a novelist of considerable acclaim. In addition to all this, Llull initiated the cult of the Virgin and provided the philosophical underpinning for the doctrines of the Immaculate Conception and the Assumption. There is a stained glass window in one of the churches in Palma, the capital of Majorca. It shows St. Francis and St. Dominic watching with approval as Ramón Llull in purple robes and Duns Scotus in blue, announce their doctrine of the Virgin. "I revere Llull," writes James Michener, "because in his day he saw the interlocking nature of the world and was willing to sacrifice his life to help achieve unity. To him the Mediterranean was infinitely larger than the Atlantic and the Pacific are to me, yet he went forth to all the shores, preaching one message, 'He who loves not, lives not'."

Llull lived well into his eighties. He died in the year 1316, perhaps, as many believe (particularly Franciscans) as a martyr. *Encyclopedia Britannica* states that irate Muslims stoned him to death outside the city walls of Bougie, in Africa. *The Catholic Encyclopedia* claims that he was stoned to death by Saracens during his visit to Tunisia. This great figure, *Doctor Illuminatus*, as he is called, is entombed on the Island of Majorca, his birthplace, in the convent dedicated to another troubadour and exuberant Christian, St. Francis of Assisi.

Youthfulness

"Virtues and viruses" presents a thought provoking juxtaposition of terms. If we had our wits with us, we would always chose virtues and eschew viruses. Yet, we do not always have our wits with us, and while our wits are on holiday we are apt to reject the difficult virtue while disposing ourselves to receiving the available virus. It takes effort to acquire a virtue; we need only to be exposed to a virus in order to be infected by it.

When Dostoevsky submitted his manuscript, *Crime and Punishment*, for publication, he included a brief synopsis of the novel in a covering letter. In this way, he informed the publisher that his story was about a university student who "had submitted to certain strange, incomplete ideas which float on the wind." It was an apt description not only of his book, but also of what happens to so many "victims" of higher education who fall prey to the attraction of a less than adequate idea.

Such "strange, incomplete ideas" continue to float on the wind and continue to infect the minds of the very university students who pride themselves in being able to "think for themselves." Ideas of this type are like viruses, but they are more insidious. By entering the mind and influencing one's actions, they can have an adverse effect on the whole person. "If the eye is worthless, the whole body will be in full darkness" (Mt 6:23; Luke 11:34).

The philosopher Alfred North Whitehead has remarked that "the deepest definition of Youth is, Life as yet untouched by tragedy . . . Quick pleasure and quick pain, quick laughter and quick tears, quick absence of care, and quick diffidence, quick courage and quick fear, are conjointly characters of youth. In other words, immediate absorption in its own occupations." Yet Professor Whitehead is by no means cynical about youth.

"The finest flower of youth," he adds, "is to know the lesson in advance of the experience, undimmed." Youthfulness, in its most virtuous attire, is vitality that is not marred by presumption. Gordon B. Hinckley has written a book entitled, *Standing for Something: 10 Neglected Virtues That Will Heal Our Hearts and Homes* (Times Books, 2000). In his chapter, "Making a Case for *Morality*," he provides a poignant account of two university students, deeply infected by one of these "strange, incomplete ideas," who came to his office with their tale of woe. The two were engaged and had been looking forward to their wedding day with great anticipation. Now, through tears, they related their sad and unforeseen situation. The girl's untimely pregnancy meant that the couple would get married much sooner than planned, and under considerably less jubilant circumstances. The thought of abortion crossed their minds, but they eventually rejected it. But it would be necessary for them to compromise their education plans. "We were sold short," the young man lamented. "We've cheated one another," sobbed his fiancée. She explained how they submitted to the idea that *virtue is hypocrisy*. Now they were suffering from the realization that the absence of virtue is not spontaneity and freedom, but misery and regret.

The notion that "virtue is hypocrisy" is a curious one. Surely hypocrisy, the mere pretense of virtue, is not itself a virtue. We do well to avoid hypocrisy. But the way to avoid this universally detested vice is precisely through virtue.

Hypocrisy is a species of pride. It is a way of pretending to be better than we know ourselves to be. Its natural antidote is *humility*. But humility is a virtue. The mere semblance of virtue may illustrate hypocrisy. Yet to think of virtue only as an outward pretense is to have a strange and incomplete understanding of virtue. Real virtue is inward and enables us to be more genuine. Its purpose is not to make us gloat and be proud of its possession, but rather to help us to love more effectively. Refusal to cultivate virtue is not the way to avoid hypocrisy. Indeed, in the absence of virtue, hypocrisy flourishes. The engaged couple, unfortunately, had a woefully incomplete notion of virtue. They thought it was pretense, whereas in reality, it is essence.

Try as we may, we cannot fully deny the value of virtuousness. We sign our letters, "sincerely" and bid each other to "take care." We bemoan the lack of "integrity" in the business world and praise the athlete who shows "determination." Our stereos must have "hi-fidelity," and a major insurance company calls itself "Prudential." And vice, which continues to pay homage to virtue, feels the need to disguise itself in virtuous raiment. Thus we have abortion for "compassion," and euthanasia for "mercy," while even members of the Mafia pride themselves on being "loyal," and "courageous." Hypocrisy may be a mockery of virtue, but in its own way pays it a lavish compliment.

Virtue is primarily an interior possession. Its primary function is to facilitate the expression of our love. Without virtue, love remains dormant and unexpressed. As we express love through virtue, virtue takes on an outward demeanor. The caring heart manifests itself outwardly, as does kindness, courtesy, and all the other sundry virtues.

According to the incomplete notion of virtue, it is just an outer appearance, without substance or foundation. Thus it is a sham, and the bearer of such a vitiated form of virtue is a hypocrite. We fear hypocrisy and the stern rebukes it earns. As a result, we avoid its apparent cause — virtue itself. Such is the trendy, but simplistic idea of virtue.

It should be apparent that the person who avoids virtue because he fears that it will turn him into a hypocrite is more concerned about public criticism than personal authenticity. We must *dare* to be virtuous, even at the risk of seeming to be hypocrites. It is for this reason that some thinkers, Winston Churchill among them, have come to believe that courage is the mother of all virtues. Courage need not be associated with the battlefield. It is present in the individual who, knowing that he is not a saint, is nonetheless willing to expose himself to the accusation of being a hypocrite.

Of course, it is better to be falsely accused of hypocrisy than to be rightly accused of moral cowardice. We do not avoid vices, such as hypocrisy, simply by dodging them. The person who imagines that he is above hypocrisy has really fallen into a deeper recess of pride. Only through virtue can one avoid the vice of hypocrisy, though not necessarily its charge. But then, the virtuous person is more interested in doing good than in having an unsullied reputation.

Reverend Hinckley's penitent university students felt cheated by the incomplete idea of virtue that was floating on the wind. They began to realize, though via the "school of hard knocks," that virtue is for the stout-hearted, indeed, for those brave souls who persist in doing good in the face of opposition and misjudgment. Christ himself remained virtuous under the assault of humiliation and public ridicule. He is our model.

Finally, youthfulness is resilience. We hope that Hinckley's students and many others who have succumbed to similar temptations will bounce back and live virtuous lives. Youthfulness has yet another endearing quality. It is the readiness to receive, deep within the heart, appeals to lofty ideals. Young people are most receptive to images of virtuous conduct and are eager to pay the price their embodiment exacts. They also believe, most ardently, in love. And to cite Whitehead once more, "Youth is peculiarly liable to the vision of that Peace which is the harmony of the soul's activities with ideal aims that lie beyond any personal satisfaction."

Zeal

Zeal is the virtue that breeds the greatest amount of distrust. There are chiefly two reasons for this. One is historical, the other contemporary. We look with dark suspicion upon those Christians of yore whose zeal was unaccompanied by moderation, prudence, or even common sense. The zeal of the Crusaders springs to mind. So *over*zealous were so many Christians and non-Christians in the past that the words *zealot* and *zealotry* came to denote vice. A "zealot" is taken to be a fanatic. "Zealotry" is fanaticism put into action.

In our present era, perhaps to give ourselves a wide margin of safety so that we do not lapse into zealotry and become zealots, we tend to avoid zeal altogether. Unfortunately, the absence of a virtue creates a moral vacuum that is quickly filled by a vice. In this instance, the vice that rushes in is *sloth*. This commonly misunderstood vice is really the indisposition or reluctance to have any interest in spiritual realities.

These two reasons for explaining our distrust of zeal may very well be conjoined. We overreact to our fear of being as zealous as zealots of the past and, as a consequence, provide room in our souls for sloth. As we become seduced by sloth, we become even more suspicious of zeal.

An instructive embodiment of sloth is the popular TV character that Jerry Seinfeld plays in his eponymous sit-com. Compared with the sheer zaniness of the characters who surround him, Gerry seems quite normal. But this is because our own vice, sloth, is difficult to recognize by a mass audience that is infected with the same disease and has come to accept it as normal. The Gerry character is non-religious, has no room for prayer in his life, dislikes opera, museums, reading, babies, everyone outside his small coterie of three friends, and fears commitment to any member of the opposite sex to the point of moral paralysis. His indisposition or reluctance to pursue any spiritual pleasures makes him a nearly ideal incarnation of the vice of sloth. The program's real joke is on the mass audience that cannot recognize its own sloth in the character it heartily accepts.

Nonetheless, zeal is a genuine virtue. "Zeal," as St. Thomas Aquinas tells us, "arises from the intensity of love" (*Summa Th.* I-II, 28, 4) and cites the authorities of both the New and Old Testaments: "With zeal I have been zealous in the Lord of hosts" (3 Kings 19:14); "The zeal of Thy house hath eaten me up" (John 2:17). In another text, Aquinas speaks of zeal that centers around virtuous goods as being praiseworthy (*Summa Th.* II-II, 36, 3) and cites St. Paul: "Be zealous for spiritual gifts" (1 Cor 14:1).

Aquinas himself well exemplifies the virtue of zeal. The Angelic Doctor, as we know, produced in his brief lifespan of forty-nine years a stupendous amount of writing. His prodigious literary output is all the more remarkable given the fact that he spent a great deal of time praying, teaching, and traveling. We could not begin to understand how he could be as prolific as he was without taking into consideration his zeal for truth.

Zeal for the truth is not a common virtue in out time. We tend to be tepid about the truth and enthusiastic about putting people down who dare show the slightest interest in the truth. We think of university teaching as interpreting "research" and analyzing "studies." For Aquinas, however, his role as a teacher was animated by his zeal for truth and his zeal for imparting truth on the hearts of his students.

At one time, a young novice submitted to Aquinas no less than thirty-six questions. The questions were poorly formulated and the neophyte had the temerity to request answers within four days. Aquinas could legitimately have excused himself, given more important matters that occupied his time. Yet he not only supplied the answers, but also reformulated the questions more precisely. In addition, he completed his assignment within the requested time limit.

No doubt the zeal that animated Aquinas affected many of his readers. There is an erroneous legend that Martin Luther burned a copy of Aquinas' *Summa Theologica* along with the papal bull in the marketplace at Wittenberg. The truth of the matter, as Josef Pieper explains in *The Silence of Saint Thomas*, makes a far more telling point. Although Luther intended to burn a copy of the *Summa*, he could not locate one since he could not find anyone who was willing to part with his copy.

Zeal begets zeal. We should not be fearful of the virtue of zeal. It springs from love and does not exclude moderation. It fires our passion to a flame and enables us to be more effective, productive, and alive.

APPENDIX

Profiles in Courage

From
Abraham Lincoln to Louis Zamperini

Abraham Lincoln

In 1996, while campaigning in California, President Clinton commented that the celebrated phrase, "that government of the people, by the people, and for the people," was enshrined in the United States *Constitution*. When this rather embarrassing inaccuracy was brought to his attention, Clinton "corrected" himself, saying that it was located, rather, in the *Declaration of Independence*.

The truth of the matter, as every student of American history should know, is that these oft-repeated words were first spoken in 1863 at Gettysburg by Abraham Lincoln. Clinton's double *faux pas* did not stand in the way of his re-election. In an atmosphere where image and style count far more than truth and substance, his twin slips where a media non-event (as opposed to Dan Quayle's alleged misspelling of "potato"). Throughout his second term as president of the world's most powerful nation, it became undeniable even to his staunchest supporters, that Clinton had little regard for the truth. If democracy is "that government of the people, by the people, and for the people," would there be any need for truth? If democracy is simply the *will* of the people, then isn't truth simply irrelevant? In fact, truth, at times, is an obstacle. It is impractical, inexpedient, and inconvenient. Clinton's version of democracy begins with freedom, though with such an amorphous beginning, it really has no place to go. There is a prevailing sense in America that the best guarantor of freedom is a form of democracy that is unencumbered by truth. Freedom, according to many Americans, is most perfectly itself when it is disentangled from the last remnant of truth. Clinton's reference to Lincoln's *Gettysburg Address* may have been a more serious oversight, even an offense to the mind and heart of America's sixteenth president, inasmuch as it identified democracy with the will of the people, rather than basing it on certain truths that would be perilous to ignore.

On another occasion, a year or two prior to his inhabiting the White House, Lincoln said, "As I would not be a slave, so I would not be a master. This expresses my idea of democracy. Whatsoever differs from this, to the extent of the difference, is not democracy."

Lincoln's astute comment embraces a fundamental truth, namely, the equality under God of all human beings. Slavery, whether from the point of view of the slave or the master, is a denial of the fundamental truth of that proposition. The Civil War was fought in defense of a truth. At Gettysburg, Lincoln expressed the fervent hope that the soldiers who died there did not die in vain and that we, the living, must dedicate ourselves "to the unfinished work which they who fought here have thus far so nobly advanced."

This "work" is the building and preserving of democracy, but one anchored in the truth of the brotherhood of man. Truth, therefore, is antecedent; freedom is consequent. Truth is primary; freedom is the fulfilling atmosphere in which the truth of man flourishes. In the absence of truth, there can be no flourishing of the human being. When truth is disregarded, freedom becomes, as Jacques Maritain has said, "but that amorphous impulse surging out of the night which is but a false image of liberty." Aquinas has pointed out in his work *On Truth* (*De Veritate*), that "the entire root of liberty is constituted in reason," and that it is reason that discerns the truth of things ("*Totius libertatis radix est in ratione constituta*").

Lincoln's understanding that freedom is meaningful only when it is rooted in the truth of man is encapsulated in the Gospel words, "You shall know the truth, and the truth shall make you free" (John 8:32). The unalterable fact that truth is not only primary, but indispensable, does not mean that it is always agreeable. "God offers to every mind," Ralph Waldo Emerson has reminded us, "its choice between truth and repose." Mounting the bathroom scale can be a breathless ascent, because the anxious weight-watcher knows that this simple piece of machinery tells the truth. But the disconcerting truth that one is overweight may be exactly what is needed if exercising and dieting are to follow. The freedom that health offers may be preceded by the unpleasant truth that one is carrying around excessive poundage.

It is precisely because truth is often disagreeable, unpleasant, and unpalatable, that love for truth is a virtue. The truth, and no substitute, shall make us free. But if we have not cultivated the virtue that gives us the strength to love truth, we cannot begin our advance toward freedom.

In a climate of racism, it may be painful (if not politically inexpedient) to recognize the truth of the equal humanity of all races. Yet, it is undeniable that there can be no human progress without recognizing, honoring, and implementing fundamental truths about man. In a climate of "choice," it may be painful to recognize the truth of the humanity of the unborn. Clinton wanted abortions to be "safe, legal, and rare." To Lincoln's everlasting credit, he did not want slavery to be "safe, legal, and rare."

The politically charged atmosphere of today's world continues to discourage people from recognizing certain truths. The truth of the unborn human being is today's challenge to the true democrat. Lincoln castigated the democrats of his time for tolerating, even advocating slavery. He was not willing to comply with a "pro-choice" view of slavery because it violated a fundamental truth that imperiled both human beings as well as a nation. Lincoln was committed to the "self-evident truth" that "all men are created equal" which Jefferson had inscribed in the

Declaration of Independence. He had no patience with attempts to compromise that truth and understood clearly where such compromises would lead. "As a nation we began by declaring that all men are created equal," he said. "We now practically read it, 'All men are created equal except the Negroes.' Soon it will read, 'All men are created equal except Negroes and foreigners and Catholics.' When it comes to this I should prefer emigrating to some country where they make no pretense of loving liberty, to Russia, for instance, where despotism can be taken pure and without the base alloy of hypocrisy."

He emphasized that the proposition, 'a house divided against itself cannot stand,' "is a truth of all human experience." Christ, in admonishing the Pharisees, had said, "Every kingdom divided against itself is brought to desolation, and every city or house divided against itself will not stand." Lincoln averred that this statement has been true for "six thousand years," which may be taken to mean, as long as there have been human beings able to discern this incontrovertible truth. Before delivering his speech in which he used the image of a house divided against itself, he solicited the opinions of several of his colleagues. One listened carefully and characterized it as a "damned fool utterance"; another contended that it was "ahead of its time"; and still another insisted that it would drive away a good many voters from the Democrats ranks. Despite the adverse comments of all those who listened to his words, Lincoln remained undeterred. "The time has come when these sentiments should be uttered," he said to them. "And if it is decreed that I should go down because of this speech, then let me go down linked to the truth — let me die in the advocacy of what is just and right."

Lincoln was open to criticism without losing sight of his firmness of purpose. To one dissenter who followed the president into his executive office, Lincoln proudly stated, "If I had to draw a pen across my record, and erase my whole life from sight, and I had one poor gift or choice left as to what I should save from wreck, I should choose that speech and leave it to the world unerased."

Lincoln's greatness as a political leader lay in the fact that not only did he recognize that freedom cannot flower except in the soil of truth, but that he had enough virtue—his love for truth—to stand by his convictions in the full face of political opposition.

Love for truth is not a common virtue. It is believed by many to be almost completely absent from the world of politics. Yet, even if this were the case, it does not diminish the primary significance of this virtue. Truth is what unites us, what brings us in touch with our reality, what gives meaning and direction to our lives, and what makes us free in the most important sense of the word. If politics is an object of cynicism, it is because it is perceived as not resting on a basis of truth. If politicians are vilified, it is because their commitment to truth is forever being compromised.

The primary significance of a love for truth has been a favorite theme of Pope John Paul II. "Let us seek the truth about Christ and about his Church! He writes in his *Agenda for the Third Millennium.* "Let us love the Truth, live the Truth, proclaim the Truth! O Christ, show us the Truth. Be the only Truth for us.

Johnny Unitas

His name sounded like a rallying-cry for team unity: "Johnny Unitas" (Unite Us). It was a moniker seemingly designed by a Hollywood script writer. Yet, as if it were his destiny, he could not have been more worthy of this most auspicious appellation.

While Cardinal William H. Keeler, archbishop of Baltimore, officiated at his funeral at the Cathedral of Mary Our Queen (Sept. 17, 2002), a plane flew overhead carrying a red-lettered banner reading "Unitas We Stand." 2,2000 people packed the church, some arriving as early as 4:00 am, to pay tribute to a man who, in the Cardinal's words, "led and touched others by his integrity and loyalty." Frank Gitschier, Unitas' former coach at the University of Louisville, was the first to speak. He referred to his hero as "the most accessible legend I've ever heard of," a man who "always had his priorities right: God, family and job." Journalists Anderson and Reinharz praised him as "a devout and temperate Catholic who lived [with his family] in the Baltimore suburbs – the very model of civility and respectability." Unitas left behind his wife and two daughter, and his six sons, who served as pallbearers. The words of William Wordsworth provide a fitting epitaph to the life and legend that is Johnny Unitas:

> One in whom persuasion and belief
> Had ripened into faith, and faith became
> A passionate intuition.

Unitas was born May 7, 1933 in Pittsburgh. His father died when Johnny was 5, and his mother raised her four children by herself, supporting them by working at two jobs. At St. Justin's, a small Catholic high school, Unitas played halfback and end until he replaced the injured starting quarterback early in his junior year. It was during his high school years that Unitas accidentally shot himself in the finger while cleaning a .38 revolver. The mishap left him unable to bend the first joint of the index finger of this throwing hand. Nonetheless, his gridiron performance in his senior year drew some attention from colleges.

Unitas wanted to play football for Notre Dame. Another Lithuanian, like himself, Moose Krause (Edward Kraucianas) had become a legend at that school, earning All-America honors both in basketball as well as football. Notre Dame passed on the aspiring quarterback, believing that Unitas, at 139 pounds, was too light. Other schools ignored him. The University of Pittsburgh offered him a scholarship, but Unitas failed the school's entrance exam.

Frank Gitschier, the University of Louisville coach took an interest in Unitas. After he promised Unitas' mother that her son would go to Mass every Sunday and would graduate, she agreed to let him attend Louisville. "It was no great recruiting coup," Gitschier later confessed, "we got Johnny U. because no one else wanted him."

The Pittsburgh Steelers drafted Unitas in the ninth round in 1955. He played none of the team's five exhibition games and was released without even throwing a single pass. An Associated Press photograph of Unitas did appear in newspapers across the country. It did not show him taking a snap from center, however, but explaining how to hold a football to a Chinese nun.

The next step for the ever-faithful Mr. Unitas was playing for a semi-pro team in Pittsburgh for $6 a game. At this point, his prospects for a career in football looked rather bleak. In addition, Unitas did not look at all like a football player. Noted sports journalist Frank Deford has described Unitas in rather unflattering terms: "He had stooped shoulders, a chicken breast, thin bowed legs and long, dangling arms with crooked, mangled fingers."

Weeb Ewbank, the head coach of the Baltimore Colts, however, saw something he liked about this gawky young quarterback, and signed him to a contract. By this time, Unitas has 190 pounds on his 6-1 frame. Unitas' debut was a shaky one. His first pass was intercepted and returned for a touchdown. He botched a handoff on his next play resulting in a fumble recovered by the opposition.

Legends are made of sterner stuff. There had been enough setbacks and deterrents in Unitas' life up to this point to induce him to abandon his dream and try a different career track. Yet, despite the discouragements, his faith was still ripening.

He threw 9 touchdowns in his rookie year, including one in the season finale that started his record 47-game streak. His 55.6% completion mark was a rookie record. The next season he threw for 2,550 yards and 24 touchdowns, and was named Most Valuable Player.

His career spanned 18 years. He set 22 NFL passing records, was named Most Valuable Player of the NFL three times, and was named to the ProBowl 10 times. He became a legend. *Sports Illustrated* declares, on the basis of meticulous statistical reckoning, that Johnny Unitas is "The Best There Ever Was" (Sept. 23, 2002).

He was a legend in football. Only a legend! In life he seemed larger than legend. His faith was indeed passionate, and fully vindicated. The man with the "golden arm" had a warm and gracious heart. "Johnny U's talents were his own," writes Frank Deford, "The belief he gave us was his gift."

Dr. Donald DeMarco
Adjunct Prof.
Holy Apostles College & Seminary

Louis Zamperini

Some individuals display virtues of such heroic proportions that they overwhelm the mere chronicler, leaving him with a sense of both inadequacy and unworthiness. Yet the extraordinary story of Louis S. Zamperini cannot be told often enough because it represents an intersection between God and man that is vitally needed for a world that has either forgotten God or has failed to recognize His Providential Care.

Louis Zamperini was born on January 26, 1917 in Olean, New York. When he was a young boy, his family moved to Torrance, California, where Lou, performing for his Torrance High School track team, won every event he entered. As a junior, in 1934, he set a world Interscholastic record for his time in the mile. Two years later he ran for the United States in the Berlin Olympics.

It would be his final Olympiad. He enlisted in the military in 1941 and trained as a bombardier. The following year, he was commissioned a second lieutenant and sent to Hawaii to join the 307th Bombardment Group, 7th Air Force. While on a search mission for a B-25 that was reported to have been shot down, both engines of Zamperini's plane conked out and his dilapidated aircraft plunged into the sea.

"I swallowed gasoline and hydraulic fluid," Zamperini would later report, "and I was bursting to get some air. I could see no way out." Trapped underwater by some cables, he was certain he was a dead man. Nearly three minutes elapsed, according to his reckoning, when suddenly a wire snapped as part of the shattered plane plunged further into the depths, and he was catapulted to the surface.

Of the 10-man crew, there were but three survivors. They lashed two rafts together, climbed atop, and hoped for rescue. But rescue planes failed to notice their flares and dye markers.

They continued to drift. Rain showers seemed to arrive miraculously at appropriate intervals. For food, they ate two small fish, three birds, four albatrosses, and the liver from a two-foot shark. "I promised God," said Lou, "that if I survive this experience, that I would seek Him and serve Him." On day 27, a Japanese patrol plane strafed them. Zamperini dove into the water, wondering if he would die by bullets or by shark bites. His two companions, too weak to move, played possum. Apparently, the ruse worked. The plane left without striking any of the three who were clinging to life, though it left 48 bullet holes in the raft.

On the 33rd day of drifting, the most severely injured of the trio died. Lou and Russ Phillips, the pilot, recited the Lord's Prayer as their companion slipped quietly into the sea. One may well ask whether the words, "Thy will be done," were ever uttered with more heartfelt nobility.

The watery ordeal lasted 47 days. Zamperini's weight dropped from 165 to 79 pounds. Yet, his trial between the blue Pacific and a scorching sun was merely a prelude to another, and perhaps more painful one. After drifting 1,500 miles, Zamperini and his companion were washed ashore on Kwajalien Island where they were picked up by a small Japanese harbor boat. This atoll was also known as Execution Island, since no prisoner had ever left there alive. For 43 days, Zamperini endured daily beatings and interrogations. He was fed insect-filled rice balls and subjected to painful chemical experimentations. Finally, when he thought the time propitious, he told his tormentors about some mock airfields the Americans had rigged up, complete with dummy aircraft made of plywood. Zamperini's artfully expressed revelation was convincing and won him some food. On the 43rd day, Zamperini was sent to Yokohama where he commenced a 2_ year internment as a prisoner of war.

Back home, it was assumed that Zamperini was dead. In New York City, the Knights of Columbus Track Meet changed the name of its showcase event, the mile, from the "Columbian Mile" to the "Lou Zamperini Memorial Mile." At the second (and final) running of this event, Lou Zamperini himself presided, functioning as the official starter. The man who returned from the dead not only appeared at his own memorial, but was even allowed to keep the money he collected from his own life insurance.

Zamperini, the Olympic athlete and War Hero, has been faithful to the promises he made while drifting on a makeshift life raft in the Pacific Ocean. He has dedicated the rest of his life to his Christian ministry and currently maintains an office at the First Presbyterian Church in Hollywood, California. He has forgiven his tormentors and has been deeply involved in bringing the message of Christ to young people.

Lou Zamperini's fidelity to a promise has brought inspiration to many. His story is told in his book, *The Devil at My Heels*, and will soon appear in a film, starring Nicolas Cage. May all who have come to know about the extraordinary exploits of Lou Zamperini extend the kind of fidelity he has witnessed through their own lives. God does nothing in vain.